Contents

Foreword

The collapse of the Soviet Union was caused in good measure by nationalism, that is, by the demands of the subject nationalities of the USSR for genuine independence and autonomy. Unified in their hostility to the Kremlin's authority, the fifteen constituent Union Republics, including the Russian republic, declared their sovereignty and began to build state institutions of their own. The demands of the titular nationalities of each republic became the dominant motifs in the programs of both Communist and non-Communist leaders. With the failure of the August 1991 putsch attempt, sovereign republics obtained their independence. Nationalism reigned supreme.

The principle of nationality that buried the Soviet Union and destroyed its empire in Eastern Europe continues to shape and reshape the configuration of states and political movements among the new countries of the vast East European–Eurasian region. The ambitions of nations grow and change, splinter and clash, much as they have in the past— only now, discordance and conflict spread too easily into armed clashes and war. The ruins of Vukovar in Croatia and the shelling of Sarajevo in Bosnia serve as terrifying examples of the quick acceleration of national conflict that already threatens—among others in the former Soviet Union—Moldavians and Russians in Transdniestria, Armenians and Azerbaijanis in Nagorno-Karabagh, and Georgians and Osetins in Southern Osetia. The two largest nations of the region, Russia and Ukraine, joust and argue over the material inheritance of the once-great Soviet superpower with the knowledge that a serious breakdown of communications or a violent miscue could trigger a conflict of catastrophic proportions.

In the shadow of potential war and violence, nations are being born and reborn. Ukrainians are studying their own language; Tajiks are learning to practice their own religion; Estonians are rewriting their constitution. Volga Tatars pursue autonomy within a genuinely federal Russian state, while Russians themselves seek to understand their role in the Eurasian land mass they have conquered, colonized, and settled over the past five centuries. Small ethnic groups in the Russian Federation and elsewhere demand control over their own territories; regionalism threatens the unity even of ethnically homogeneous regions. With the demise of the Communist supranational administrative structures of the USSR and Yugoslavia, nationalist ambitions have exploded in different directions, with their trajectories still unpredictable and malleable. This is not a case of uncorking the evil genie of national self-determination, but rather one of creating the conditions that make its evolution volatile and uncertain.

Just as the Communists underestimated the power of nationalism, Western leaders are immobilized by the changes in Eastern Europe and the former Soviet Union because of a mute incomprehension of both the accomplishments of national movements and the threats posed by their sometimes uncompromising leaders. Blinkered by their shared intellectual heritage of the Enlightenment and materialism, Marxists and liberals alike fail to appreciate the profound political impact of nationalism. With few exceptions, scholars from East and West study politics and societies from the perspective of the metropolitan centers and focus their attention on the culture of the dominant nationalities. For a variety of reasons, some more excusable than others, Sovietologists in particular were susceptible to Moscow-centered scholarship. Slavic departments were often no more than Russian departments; Kremlinology substituted for political analysis.

There were exceptions—most notably, the Studies of Nationalities (formerly Studies of Nationalities in the USSR) series edited by Wayne S. Vucinich of Stanford University and published by the Hoover Institution Press. More recently, prominent historians and social scientists—Eric Hobsbawm, Benedict Anderson, and Ernest Gellner, among them—have also turned their attention to the unanticipated resurgence of modern nationalism. But it is still strikingly rare in the literature for a scholar to apply this increasingly sophisticated theoretical understanding of nationalism, ethnopolitics, and nationality to the concrete and often unique problems of Ukrainians, Uzbeks, Russians, or Estonians, either separately or as a group of associated nations.

This book plays a critical role in providing this synthesis. Above all a history of the nationalities of the former Soviet Union, Ronald G. Suny's work here demonstrates the dynamic influence of specific Imperial and Soviet Russian historical contexts on the creation and perpetual recreation of national self-consciousness among the peoples of the region. He demonstrates that ideas of nationality are deeply embedded in these nations' understanding of their past. In turn, historical interpretation shapes the development of nationalism today and in the future. Without sacrificing the astonishing diversity of national experiences in the Russian empire and the Soviet Union, the book develops a comprehensive analysis of the relationships between nationality, modernity, and class. Suny combines methodological expertise, a thorough background in Russian and Soviet history, and recognized competence in the history and historiography of discrete non-Russian nations, especially the Georgians and Armenians. This allows him to attack the roles of nationalities in the formation, maintenance, and decline of the Soviet state with unusual clarity and nuance. Specialists and non-specialists alike will profit from the understanding of the past and future provided by his unique point of view.

Ronald G. Suny is Alex Manoogian Professor of Armenian History at the University of Michigan. This book was first presented to the Stanford community as the Donald M. Kendall Lectures in Soviet Studies. The Center for Russian and East European Studies sponsored the lectures and is honored to publish them in cooperation with the Stanford University Press.

Norman M. Naimark
Director, Center for Russian and East European Studies
Stanford University

Preface

The invitation to speak at Stanford University on the "nationality problems" in the Soviet Union gave me a welcome opportunity to collect my thoughts about a number of diverse but related issues—class and nationality identities, the role of empires and states in the making of nations, the long- and short-term causes of the failure of the Soviet experiment. The confidence of Norman Naimark and Alexander Dallin that I would be able to deliver both a historical narrative and an analysis of the formation of nations within the Russian empire and the Soviet Union, as well as a reasonable discussion of the recent cascade of events, inspired me to think about theoretical as well as more empirical problems—even to engage in a little prediction.

In February 1991, when I gave the lectures, the Soviet Union still existed, the focus of a violent political contest between those who wanted preservation of some kind of center and those who wanted dissolution into independent republics. My sense at the time was that four scenarios could be played out. The least likely was a return to the pre-

Gorbachevian order, a return to party oligarchy, centralization, and an imperial relationship between Moscow and its constituent nations. In early 1991, this scenario remained a utopian dream for many Communists who had imbibed the deeply conservative legacy of Stalinism, but it could not be realized without a coup d'état supported by the army and the police. Such a coup was indeed attempted and proved a fiasco. The popular mobilization, the loss of faith in the old ideology, and the lack of any program for the "forces of order" to restore the Soviet economy make a Stalinesque or Brezhnevian vision completely unrealistic.

A second scenario was increasingly predicted in the West and by many Soviet nationalists at the time: the breakup of the Soviet Union and the creation of 15 sovereign states. Though this would have brought the Soviet empire to an end, many pointed out that it would not necessarily lead to the triumph of democracy. In several of the non-Russian republics, authoritarian and national chauvinistic tendencies remained paramount, and the minorities that live in Georgia, Uzbekistan, Azerbaijan, or even Lithuania were fearful about their futures in countries dominated by the majority nationality. In several republics, independence soon became a cover for preservation of the old ruling elites, now the defenders of national sovereignty.

A third scenario posited the partial breakup of the Soviet Union: independence for the Baltic republics, possible unification of Moldavia with a more democratic Romania, but the unity of the three Slavic republics with Central Asia and Transcaucasia on the basis of confederation. The new, smaller Soviet Union would be a voluntary union, based on shared powers, with great internal political, cultural, and economic autonomy for the republics and regions of the new state.

The fourth scenario, related to the third but perhaps the most optimistic of all, proposed the renewal of the entire

USSR as a democratic confederation. This was, of course, Gorbachev's preferred solution, and one he might have achieved had the decaying Soviet system not been overwhelmed by the consequences of three simultaneous revolutionary processes: marketization, which led to the collapse of the command economy without an alternative in place; democratization, which undermined all forms of authority, particularly that of the political center; and decolonization, which led to the fragmentation of the Union itself and the devolution of power to the republics. The national question proved to be, as the demonstrators in Karabagh in 1988 proclaimed on their signs, a "test for *perestroika*," but it was one that Gorbachev ultimately failed. Time, unfortunately in my opinion, was not on Gorbachev's side, even if history will be.

R.G.S.

Acknowledgments

Debts, emotional and intellectual, can never fully be paid, but a scholar at least has the space to acknowledge some of those who helped along the way. Most importantly, my good friend and comrade, Geoff Eley, has been a reservoir of insights, suggestions, and support. His vast knowledge of nationalism has shaped my own understanding in ways I no longer can decipher. Other colleagues, through discussion and debate, through reading parts of the text and challenging arguments, have made significant contributions to this book of which they may be unaware. Special thanks for good comments and conversations are due to Robin Blackburn, Abe Brumberg, Moshe Lewin, Ann Stoler, Roman Szporluk, and Andrew Verner; to the members of the History department at the University of California, Irvine, where the sections on class and nationality were written; to Natalie Davis, Laura Engelstein, and the members of the Davis Center, who engaged my arguments vigorously in an extraordinary seminar; to those at the Universities of Edmonton, Minnesota,

Chicago, and North Carolina, and at Southern Methodist University, who listened and questioned; and to Alex Dallin, Terry Emmons, Scott Sagan, William and Ellen Sewell, and other friends and colleagues who exchanged ideas with me in three days of discussion at Stanford University; and, most importantly, to the members of MSG, CSST, and Affiliations at the University of Michigan, who listened, responded, and encouraged.

Bits and pieces of the lectures on which this book is based have appeared in earlier forms in collections of articles on Soviet history and politics and in the *New Left Review*.[1] Though it is impossible to say when and where certain ideas and formulations gestated, I will always remember my friend and colleague at Oberlin College, George Lanyi, whose invitation to lecture in his class on the nationality problem forced me to face the contradictions inherent in and generated by the Leninist state. George is missed by all who knew him, and his wisdom, insight, and humor are more than ever needed as the part of the world he knew best moves through uncharted waters. Finally, Norman Naimark, the proverbial friend in need from the time we first met, made a singular contribution to this whole endeavor, from the invitation to deliver the lectures to the most careful editorial reading of the final manuscript.

Though these lectures are largely about the "constructedness" of nationality, my own interest in the "national question" in the Soviet Union, and in nationalism more generally, might be seen in a sense to have had more primordial origins. As children of Armenian parents, one born in the United States, the other in historic Armenia, my sister and I listened from an early age to the Armenian language, ate the foods of a country that had been lost, and heard stories of those from "the other side." But George and Arax Suny were somewhat unusual Armenians. They took for granted that we were simultaneously Armenians and Americans, and though they never forced on their children the stamp of ethnicity, they gave us a sense of the wonder of difference. Nationality in our family was always a voluntary matter. That appreciation of choice and imagination in constructing identity runs through this book.

The Revenge
of the Past

CHAPTER I

Rethinking Social Identities: Class and Nationality

Nationalism comes before nations. Nations do not make states and nationalism but the other way round.

—E. J. Hobsbawm, *Nations and Nationalism*

The unprecedented crisis in what was the Soviet Union today conjures up images from other Times of Troubles. From both the Left and the Right, in the West and in the embryonic republics of the late USSR, we hear ever more frequent warnings about the collapse of the economy, the disintegration of the state, and an inexorable drift into civil war. In the rush of events, historical antecedents and determinants appear dimly, often as mystifications, sometimes as analogues to predict possible futures. Rather than feeling enriched by the explosion of new information about the present and, to a lesser extent, the past, many of us are disarmed by the unexpected. History has again come to haunt us. Just when the shape of things seems clear and under control, just when guards are lowered and the inherited burdens of the past seem to have been relieved, history intrudes, often violently, reminding us of its irreducible power.

Less clearly recognized than the crisis in the country we study is the parallel crisis within Soviet studies in the West. Limited by its longtime allegiance to centrist, top-down,

Russian-biased political analyses, and seduced by ahistoric models and deductive reasoning from ideology and personality, Sovietology paid far too little attention for far too long to the non-Russian peoples, to the extrapolitical social environment, and to the particular contexts, contingencies, and conjunctures of the Soviet past. Soviet studies at times, notably during the Cold War, were concentrated so much on politics, psychology, and applied anthropology that its scholars were unable to appreciate the deep historical transformations and contradictions that both created and ultimately brought down a unique social formation.

How could so many have been so wrong about the internal dynamics of the Soviet state and society? Why did almost no one foresee the possibility of a democratic reform initiated from the very top of the Communist party? Much of Sovietological analysis had been built on a conviction that the nature of totalitarianism precluded the kind of reform initiated by Gorbachev. Distinguished historians reminded us that Russian political culture was so deeply authoritarian that an offshoot as distinctively Western as political pluralism could not appear. The West initially responded to the changes in the Soviet Union with disbelief and deep suspicion of the sincerity of the initiatives. Each turn of events, each incident of hesitation or of backsliding, seemed to confirm those suspicions.

Suspicion was replaced by the conviction that the Gorbachev reforms must fail. But the projected reasons for failure changed over time. Few understood, until it was overwhelmingly clear to all, that besides chronic economic woes, the greatest threat to both the Soviet state and its potential for reform would be the emergence of mass nationalist movements.

The very suddenness with which these movements appeared, their dimensions and durability, required from their analysts a deeper historical grounding than was generally available in the area of Soviet studies. A chasm, seldom crossed, existed between those who dealt with Russian studies proper and those who studied non-Russian peoples. The relatively neglected field of nationality studies was itself marred by nationalism and narcissism. Much of this has changed since February 1988, due to the non-Russian nationalities that organized massive and sustained oppositions, which eventually undermined Gorbachev's revolution-from-above and produced a fatal multiethnic challenge to the Kremlin's agenda for a limited *perestroika*.

Making Nations, Making Classes

Yet another divide, in this case professional and disciplinary, has separated many of the Western observers of nationalism in the former Soviet Union from scholars of nationalism and colonialism. In exploring the present dimensions and dynamics of nationalist movements in the Soviet Union, journalists and others have usually viewed current nationalisms as eruptions of long-repressed primordial national consciousnesses, as expressions of denied desires liberated by the kiss of freedom (what might be called the "Sleeping Beauty" view). This view of nationalism has been challenged in the literature on ethnicity and colonialism by the counterclaim that nationalism should be understood as a discourse that became dominant among masses of Europeans and non-Europeans only in the relatively recent historical past and as a result of social, political, and cultural developments that took place after the American and French Revolutions.[1] Furthermore, not only nationalism, but also nationality itself has been conceived as a social and "imagined" construction actively cobbled together from actual social and historical material. The intellectuals and activists who forge these constructions propose a new form of association with specific cultural and political claims, and with the participation of constituents who submerge other identities, localist or universalist, in order to accept paramount loyalty to the nation. The new emphasis on the "invented" and "constructed" nature of nationality and nationalism (what might be called the "Bride of Frankenstein" view) has had almost no resonance in Russian and Soviet studies. Yet it offers the distinct advantage of historicizing the problem of nationality formation and providing a comparative perspective on the different histories of the peoples of Russia and the USSR. In addition, nationality formation can be related to the construction of other social categories and identities that intersect nationality, most importantly class.

One of the supreme ironies of twentieth-century experience must be that nationalism's principal opponent, namely Marxism, has been both empowered by its alliances with nationalism and responsible for creating the conditions for the development of nations in the Second and Third Worlds. Marxists long maintained that modern nations resulted from the capitalist mode of production—that they were, in fact, so dependent on it that with the end of capitalism, nations themselves would begin to disappear. Marxists rejected the nationalist legitimation of independent nation-states constituted on the basis of ethnicity, claiming that nations were neither natural nor eternal and that priority must be given to class as the foundation of a future nationless society. Yet twentieth-century experience—the emergence of ethnically based states in the wake of World War I, Leninist concessions to the power of nationalism, and the degeneration of nationalism into virulent racism and expansionism in the 1930s—made unsustainable the argument that nationalism and nationality were disappearing in the solvent of economic development and social mobility. Just as Bolshevik politicians understood the need to accommodate the actual loyalties and aspirations of their citizens, so Marxist theorists had to moderate the more extreme reductions of ethnic culture and national formation to economics. Even Soviet analysts, constrained by theoretical dictates, were forced by the 1960s to recognize the independent variable of ethnic culture.

Yet by locating the development of nationality and nation in specific economic, ethnic, and social relations of subordination and dominance, the Marxist tradition at least rendered the problem of nation-making and the emergence of nationalism subject to historical analysis and, perhaps, explanation. An earlier historiography (Hans Kohn, C.J.H. Hayes) that extended back conceptually to the eighteenth-century German originators of nationalist thought (Herder, Fichte) emphasized the emotional, religious aspects of nationalist loyalties; although nationalism might be described and typologized, such a state of mind (*Nationalbewusstsein*) ultimately defied explanation.[2] The "living and active corporate will" (Kohn) that turned ethnic raw material into conscious politics was elusive and historically disconnected; its appearance seemed mysterious, even magical, and was compatible with the assumptions of nationalists that the essence of nationality was natural and eternal, and needed but the right opportunity to be fully released.

Though the Marxist classics can be faulted for reducing nationality to socioeconomic structures, much of the most significant reassessment of nationalist theory has come from attempts to rethink the relationships of nation and state, nationality and capitalism, by writers close to (or coming out of) Western Marxist traditions.[3] Beginning with Tom Nairn's influential essay on "the break-up of Britain," followed by Eric J. Hobsbawm's critical response, Geoff Eley's discussion of nationalism and social history, Miroslav Hroch's empirical investigations of the formation of national intelligentsias in Eastern Europe, and Benedict Anderson's evocation of "imagined communities," the discussion of nationalism has moved away from sterile definitions and typologies into historically grounded elaborations of the actual making of nationalities and nations.[4]

Following the lead of these writers, the "making of nations" can be seen as a process shaped by both socioeconomic and political developments, conceived and articulated in an emerging national discourse. Whatever the pre-existing communities—political, social, religious, ethnic—when people begin to believe that they can communicate more easily with some than with others, when they begin to define who is within the group and who are the "others," when they begin to gain the capacity to act in whatever "interests" they believe they share (which may be opposed to those of the "others"), the formation takes on a coherence and consciousness that allows it to act collectively. Making nationality, like making class, can be seen as a complex process of creating an "imagined community" that finds its expression in symbols, rituals, flags, songs, collective actions, and the articulation and representation of its goals. Both nationality and class have their discontents and their utopias. They seek to eliminate the former by achieving the latter. Whether they get their history right or not— and they usually do not, to paraphrase Ernest Renan—nationalities and nations are made in the active elaboration of a national tradition, the making of a usable past that underlies claims to political recognition, autonomy, sovereignty, or independence.[5]

Historicizing the Nation

The historical formation of classes and nationalities (one should try to avoid the use of terms like "the rise of" or "the emergence of," which contain an immanentist sense of a pre-existing essence) is, like other historical problems, a matter of specific contexts, particular conjunctures, and unpredictable contingencies. In Europe, the formation of classes and nationalities was related to the "great transformation" associated with industrial capitalism. The process involved building on evolving cultural, economic, or political solidarities and appropriating older traditions and discourses, which were reinterpreted and recombined.

As one of the dominant discourses of our century, nationalism has acquired the attributes of a force of nature rather than a product of history, and the argument from nature has in turn imparted an irresistible power to nationalism. Two major theorists of nation-making, Karl Deutsch and Benedict Anderson, have attempted to historicize the nation by emphasizing the importance of new forms of social communication in its formation. Deutsch conceptualized the "making" of nationality as an historical process of political integration that increases communication among the members of an ethnic group or a "people." A people, "a group of persons linked . . . by complementary habits and facilities of communication," has the ability "to communicate more effectively, and over a wider range of subjects, with members of one large group than with outsiders."[6] The increase in social communication is related by Deutsch to other processes of social change, such as urbanization, the development of markets, or the building of railroads. A progression is made from a "people" to a "nationality" ("a people pressing to acquire a measure of effective control over the behavior of its members . . . , striving to equip itself with power"), and eventually (though not necessarily) to a "nation-state."

Benedict Anderson proposed that the arrival of "print-capitalism," as he calls it, precipitated the search for new ways to link fraternity, power, and time.[7] The rise of the vernacular in publishing and in state administration required that a standardized usable language be chosen. "What, in a positive sense, made the new communities imaginable was a half-fortuitous, but explosive, interaction between a system of production and productive relations (capitalism), a technology of communications (print), and the fatality of human linguistic diversity."[8] Print-capitalism required that spoken dialects be assembled into print-languages, fewer in number and capable of being understood by larger publics. Larger, unified fields of communication were created, which later would be reinforced through state-sponsored schools, recruitment of men into armies with a single command language, and increased interaction of formerly isolated villagers in markets and towns.

Deutsch and Anderson's communication models are certainly improvements on the naturalistic idea of nationality as immanent in human relations, in the same way that kinship or family were seen as unproblematic relationships endowed by nature. But in Deutsch, the discussion of the transformative power of the social environment gives an undue primacy to social processes and structures from which meanings and understandings are then generated. Anderson's extraordinary breakthrough, in which the imaginative construction of the nation is brought into prominence, has encouraged scholars to move toward a more serious engagement with the extra-social realm of discourse and meaning. In a similar way, much of the thinking on class formation in the last several decades, particularly since the appearance of the seminal book on the making of the English working class by Edward Thompson, has supplemented an older Marxist notion of class as arising mysteriously from productive relations by introducing a more dynamic and ethnographic conception of class. For Thompson, class happens when people, "as a result of common experiences (inherited and shared), feel and articulate the identity of their interests as between themselves, and as against other[s] . . . whose interests are different from (and usually opposed to) theirs."[9] As part of that common experience, people enter or fall into historically created productive relations. Those relations make up the context and much of the content of their social experience, which may create a sense of class loyalty. Thompson again: "Class-consciousness is the way in which these experiences are handled in cultural terms: embodied in traditions, value-systems, ideas, and institutional forms. If the experience appears as determined, class consciousness does not."[10]

As powerful as his cultural notion of class is, Thompson has been criticized for replacing structural relations with experience as the principal determination from which an identity of interests (that is, class consciousness) arises. In the view of one of Thompson's most sensitive critics, experience should not be

> seen as the objective circumstances that condition identity; identity is not an objectively determined sense of self defined by needs and interests; politics is not the collective coming to consciousness of similarly situated individual subjects. Rather politics is the process by which plays of power and knowledge constitute identity and experience.[11]

Contests for power, always central to the Marxist notion of class, are not to be understood as simply derived from similar social and historic locations or experiences. Rather, it is within complex political contestations over identities and meanings, struggles understood in the language of politics, that communities of horizontal or vertical affiliation—that is, class or nationality—are formed.

Theorists and historians of class (like Thompson, Eric J. Hobsbawm, Ira Katznelson, William H. Sewell, Jr., and Gareth Stedman-Jones), as well as those of nationality (Benedict Anderson, Ernest Gellner, Geoff Eley, and Hobsbawm again), have stressed that social and cultural processes cannot be conceived simply as objective forces existing outside the given class or nationality; rather, they are mediated and shaped by the social, cultural, and linguistic experiences of individuals and groups within and without the social group. Experience, however, does not result in an unmediated way in predictable responses, but is itself discursively constituted, and the task of the historian is to investigate not only the effects of "experience," but also the meanings and identities generated in human activity.[12]

Classes and nationalities are constantly being made and remade, in a complex creation of identities that overlap, reinforce, and undermine one another. The active work of individuals, parties, newspapers, and intellectuals is key to the manufacture of the meaning given to experience on a collective level and to the creation of articulated social and national consciousness. Talking class or nationality, socialism or nationalism, is central to the generation of class or nationality from thousands of individual experiences and understandings. Understandings of ethnic and social differences, themselves always in the process of construction and contestation, are available to the intellectuals and activists who in turn privilege a particular perception of society and history and work to consolidate a social formation or political movement for the ends they consider desirable. They find, borrow, or invent the social and ethnic "traditions" they need. They revive, refine, and pass down rhetoric, symbols, and rituals that soon appear to have a naturalness and authenticity that originates deep in history and possesses clear legitimacy for shaping the future.[13]

The Czech historian Miroslav Hroch has been particularly helpful in recovering the important constitutive role of the early nationalists in the generation of nationalism. Basing his conclusions on close empirical investigations of smaller Eastern European peoples, Hroch proposes a three-stage evolution of nationalist movements. Phase A occurs when a small number of scholars first demonstrate "a passionate concern . . . for the study of the language, the culture, the history of the oppressed nationality." Phase B involves "the fermentation-process of national consciousness," during which a larger number of patriotic agitators diffuse national ideas.

Phase C is the full national revival, when the broad masses have been swept up into the nationalist movement.[14] Hroch, like those who have worked on the "invention of tradition" in the process of nation-building, underscores the active intellectual and political intervention of educated strata in the process of national formation.

The Prehistory of Modern Nations and Classes

The investigation of nationality and class formation is an exploration of the social and political developments that made possible certain kinds of communication, as well as the intellectual and linguistic interpretations that gave particular meanings to individual and collective experiences. Scholarship on national movements in the Russian empire continues to concentrate almost exclusively on the intellectual and political leaders and institutions of the non-Russian peoples. As a result, there is little sense of the stages of development of different national movements, and a regrettable tendency to compress the experience of the whole nationality into that of the patriotic intelligentsia, as if the two were identical. Like the ambitions and actions of workers, which in an older labor historiography were often collapsed into those of trade unionists and socialists, the actions and understandings of ethnic masses have been equated or confused with the activities of their leaders, the writings of their intellectuals, or the votes of bodies that claim to represent them.

Although fully mobilized classes and nationalities are relatively modern phenomena, they did not spring full-blown from the imaginations of their self-designated leaders and theorists. The constructed nature of nationality or national consciousness, class or class consciousness should not be taken to mean that these are "artificial" entities and therefore are illegitimate in some sense. An "imagined community," one colleague reminded me, is not an imaginary community.[15]

Modern nationality may be rooted in pre-existing cultural milieus (or "ethnie," in Anthony D. Smith's terms) that have existed since the earliest recorded human societies and "have vied or colluded with other forms of community—of city, class, religion, region—in providing a sense of identity among populations and in inspiring in them a nostalgia for their past and its traditions."[16] Distinguished by the collective names by which they were known to themselves and to others, these ethnolinguistic or ethnoreligious communities shared a common myth of descent, some notions of history, usually a language and religion, a sense of solidarity or kinship, and often an association with a specific territory.[17] Hobsbawm refers to this "feeling of collective belonging" on which nationality and nationalism would be built as "proto-nationalism."[18]

Though many ethnolinguistic or ethnoreligious communities disappeared through assimilation or through conquest in war, warfare between states powerfully enhanced and solidified a sense of ethnicity. So compelling are these identities in some cases that certain ethnoreligious groups that have lost their states, and even their homelands, like the Jews and the Armenians, have survived for millennia. Here, unusually powerful constructions of religious uniqueness and destiny, of being a chosen people or of playing a special role in the economy of human salvation, encouraged resistance to assimilation or conversion, even in the diaspora.

Although the generation of nationalism should be distinguished from the formation of nationality, the two phenomena are intimately related. Nationality, in my view, is the modern, secular form of ethnicity with a degree of coherence and consciousness that enables its members to be mobilized for national political goals. Modern nationalities, which are usually larger, territorially more dispersed communities than the ethnies out of which they may have grown, have been successfully organized and mobilized by the work of intellectuals and politicians and can put forth cultural and political demands that may include autonomy, sovereignty, and independence. Though ethnie and nationality might be distinguished in any number of ways—size, attachment to territory, secular versus religious identity, "soft" versus "hard" boundaries—the most fundamental difference is not some "objective" characteristic internal to the group, but rather the discursive universe in which it operates and realizes itself. A modern nationality, with all its familiar qualities and political claims—popular sovereignty, ethnicity as a basis for political independence, and a claim on a particular piece of real estate—are only possible within the modern (roughly post-American revolution) discourse of nationalism. Whatever Greeks in the classical period, or Armenians in the fifth century, were, they could not be nations in the same sense as they would be in the age of nationalism. The discourses of politics of earlier times must be understood and respected in their own particularity and not submerged in understandings yet to come.

Which discourse finds resonance among social groups and becomes dominant depends on the environment that "enlighteners," "patriots," "radicals," or others find or create and whether it is receptive and exploitable. But whether it is the discourse of class or of nation, of supranational religion or of subnational regionalism, the political and intellectual actors can only borrow, adapt, and reproduce the discourses available to them—or, in rarer instances, create from available material a new discursive synthesis.

Nationalism (here following Anthony D. Smith) is a doctrine that at its core holds that humanity is divided into nations, that loyalty to nations overrides all other loyalties, that the source of all political power lies within the collectivity of the nation, and that nations are fully realized only in sovereign states.[19] In an extreme but very suggestive definition of nationalism, Elie Kedourie provocatively claims,

> Nationalism is a doctrine invented in Europe at the beginning of the nineteenth century. . . . Briefly, the doctrine holds that humanity is naturally divided into nations, that nations are known by certain characteristics which can be ascertained, and that the only legitimate type of government is national self-government.[20]

Several influential theorists, among them Ernest Gellner, John Breuilly, and Eric Hobsbawm, define nationalism as "primarily a principle which holds that the political and national unit should be congruent."[21] Though this definition accounts only for a subset of the varieties of nationalist ideologies and narrows excessively the common understanding of nationalism, it has the advantage of underlining the centrality of political interests and the goal of nationhood expressed in statehood, which is found in the nationalist discourses of the last two centuries. These are distinctly modern notions that, whatever their historical connections to earlier conceptions of statehood and uniqueness, are only fully realized when a discourse of nationalism has been articulated.

However artificial the doctrine may have appeared in the work of early intellectuals, with the material, social, cultural, and political transformations of the nineteenth and twentieth centuries, nationalism gained an enormous resonance—first among a large number of educated people, then within the broad populace—until it promised to displace all rival forms of loyalty and identity. Though two hundred years ago the claim of nationality to replace older ideas of legitimation was challenged by conservatives like Lord Acton, in our century it has become the hegemonic political discourse of sovereignty and the unavoidable language of those who want to play the game of statehood. The discourse of nationalism gave a particular shape and meaning to historic social and cultural developments, and the modern representation of ethnicity in Europe became that associated with the nationalist discourse. Nationalism did not arise spontaneously from prior existing nationality, as most nationalists would have it, nor was it the "false consciousness" of the great transformation from precapitalism to postcapitalism, as some Marxists would argue. Nationalism both contributed to the formation of nationality (in Hroch's Phase B), which often in Europe (but not always) occurred on the basis of evolving ethnolinguistic or ethnoreligious communities, and evolved itself to become the political expression of mobilized nationalities (in Phase C).

Just as protonationalities (ethnies, peoples) were constantly forming and reproducing in premodern times, so horizontal social formations (strata, estates, classes), related to particular regimes of production and legal structures, were generated. They maintained a degree of demographic stability and created their own institutions and organizations in the context of the historical discourses that gave them sense, reason, and purpose. Yet, again, the long revolution of capitalism and the attendant formation of bureaucratic states provided the principal context for two opposing articulations of society and history, one based on horizontal affiliations (class), the other on vertical ones (nationality). As nationalist intellectuals homogenized the differences within their ethnic populations and drew vertical lines of distinction between themselves and the "others," a competing discourse based on new social differentiations and older traditions challenged vertical allegiances and emphasized horizontal class solidarities.

Two scenarios now might be envisioned for the emergence of fully conscious classes or nationalities. The first separates analytically the preconscious class or ethnicity from its more mature stage. A class in itself or an ethnie or a people exists as a collection of persons with shared characteristics—a similar position in the production process or shared linguistic and cultural practices. With the development of the modern world, these classes and peoples coalesce into more coherent formations, ready in time to take action in their own "interests."[22] In this reading, the social context in which workers or ethnies find themselves leads to certain understandable responses. In the classical Marxist understanding, the full realization of working-class interests is a product (somewhat magically) of capitalist development and ultimately requires revolution and the overthrow of capitalism. In the nationalist understanding, the nationality's unequal relationship with an imperial power pushes it to realize its full interests, which include the achievement of nationhood, perhaps ultimately state sovereignty.

A second scenario is more suspicious of the teleology, determinism, and failure to account for agency implicit in the first. Rather than positing a strict distinction between classes or nationalities "in themselves" and "for themselves," this approach conceives of these formations at all stages of development as being constituted by myriad social and intellectual processes, by various forms of collective action. But at different times they are represented and interpreted differently. Classes and nationalities, like older social formations, are at all stages the consequences of struggles, victories, and defeats that define and bind, differentiate and reject certain kinds of understanding.[23] Full modern nationalism is merely one phase—the latest or current one, with its own special characteristics—of the development of contested cultural communities, but it is neither the only stage in which self-realization takes place nor the end of the evolution of national formations.[24] Likewise, classes in the earlier stages of formation are far from inert demographic conglomerates waiting to achieve (or receive, in the Leninist version) enlightenment; rather, they are active in their own constitution, and they vary in their makeup and self-representation, often borrowing and reshaping older traditions and languages to meet new situations. The working class, for example, which even in later stages hardly fits the model of full proletarianization envisioned by Marx, is never really fully "made." Socialist class-consciousness in this scenario represents merely a moment only occasionally realized in social development and existing under very particular historical conditions (and usually only at the level of cities and regions, not as a nationwide phenomenon).[25]

Whatever the degree of cohesion and consciousness of classes and peoples before their mass mobilization, they represent authentic points of development. Rather than being viewed as premature, adolescent, or primitive, they should be appreciated in their full constellation of initiatives, influences, and responses. An ethnoreligious formation (such as the ancient Jews or the medieval Armenians) was not yet a modern nationality with its self-conscious sense of the value of its ethnic and secular cultural (in contrast to religious) traditions and with consequent political claims to territory, autonomy, or independence that arose from a more modern discourse authorizing the claims of nationality to self-determination. But earlier histories of classes and nations should be read not simply as prehistories, but as varied historical developments whose trajectories remained open-ended.

I do not mean to suggest that class and nationality are the same kind of formation, only that in their generation and evolution they are both constituted politically. The weight given to various inputs—production, culture, biology—will differ in the histories of these categories. Seeing them as fluid, provisional identities allows a less dichotomous appreciation of the correspondences between them. The boundaries of certain ethnicities and social classes, as in Eastern Europe and Russia, suggest that productive relations also play a part in the making of nationality and nationalism. And if one accepts the proposition that languages, ethnic relations, and social geography have profound effects on class cohesion, consciousness, and the ability (or inability) to act collectively, the overlapping of class and nationality becomes more obvious.

In this approach, neither nationality nor class is "objective" in the sense of existing outside the constitutive practices of its members and its opponents. But although it might be thought of as "subjective" (in the sense that it exists when it is perceived to exist), the "existence" of class or nationality is historically related to the actual practice of human actors, both individually and collectively, within changing social and discursive frameworks. Historical and social locations, themselves constantly being constituted, make up the context in which class or nationality identification is constructed. Those identities may be ambiguous or combined with other identities, though they are likely to be reinforced and simplified in political confrontations, which demand less-ambiguous choices.[26] They may be built around core ethnic solidarities or compound ethnic groupings, around shared positions in the mode of production or a number of quite distinct positions (e.g., artisans and factory workers). It is not always easy to predict which social or ethnic ingredients will become part of a class or nationality; it depends on the specific political conjunctures and discourses involved in its making.

The formation of class and nationality should be understood to be a contingent and historically determined occurrence rather than the working out of a natural or historical logic or a sociological derivative. One must discard the comfortable notion (for socialists) that a militant, revolutionary, class-conscious working class was the natural outcome of the history of labor. One must also throw away the dearly held conviction (of nationalists and their supporters) that an independent, sovereign (and fairly homogeneous) nation-state was the natural and inevitable outcome of nationalism and the national struggle. Classes and ethnicities in one form or another exist in various historical periods, but their political claims are the specific products of historically derived discourses of our own times.

CHAPTER 2

National Revolutions and Civil War in Russia

Because many of the peoples of the Russian empire, after five or six decades of Soviet or independent development, had forged national-cultural identities with established state structures and powerful nationalist political discourses, historians have often viewed the revolutionary years as if that future had already existed in 1917. The nationalist representation of an essential if concealed national consciousness, ever present and ready to emerge when opportunity knocked, seemed borne out by subsequent events and was easily read back into an earlier age. The appeal of this nationalist construction, its success in mobilizing populations at the end of the 1980s in political struggles for sovereignty, has obscured a much more complex, if less melodramatic, story of nation-building, and even nationality formation, which for many peoples of the empire belongs more appropriately to the Soviet period than to the years before the civil war.[1] The dramatic narratives of uneven evolution from ethnic and religious communities into conscious nationalities and the complex relationship with class formations—all taking place in the swirling vortex of war and economic collapse—need to be recovered.

Unless one simply assumes that ethnicity always and everywhere has a greater power than class, or vice versa, the particular contexts in which one or the other emerges paramount must be part of the story. How the larger political context—public policies, oppressive laws, public education, recruitment into armies, interstate conflicts, and other political interventions from states and powerful elites—contributes to the kinds of discourse that find resonance in social groups is a question that has to be particularized in microstudies of class and nationality formation. Access to state institutions or isolation from them profoundly influences the generation of identities. Moreover, the direction from which the major danger to a social formation comes—from above, in the form of state oppression, or from below, in the claims of other classes, or from outside, in a foreign threat or alien ethnicity—determines what solidarities are forged. The intensity with which commitment to class or nationality (or, indeed, to religion, region, gender, or generation) is felt at a given time is highly dependent on specific political relations and the depth and ferocity of the social and political conflicts of the moment.

Class and Nationality in the Russian Empire

Looking through the exclusive prisms of Marxism or nationalism, theorists and political activists in the late nineteenth and early twentieth centuries structured their understandings of social reality and political antagonisms by positing a strict division between class and nationality. The rival discourses of nationalism and Marxism radically simplified the complex, overlapping relationships between ethnicity and social structures and limited each movement's appeal among significant populations.

As many writers have pointed out, in Eastern Europe and the Russian empire, class and ethnic identities existed simultaneously and with little separation. Sometimes ethnic loyalties were paramount, often preventing or delaying class solidarity; at other times horizontal social links thwarted vertical ethnic integration. In particular configurations, ethnicity and class coincided, tying specific groups together in opposition to other ethnically homogeneous groups. In central Transcaucasia, for example, Georgian nobles and peasants, who shared an ethnic culture and values based on rural, precapitalist traditions, faced an entrepreneurial Armenian urban middle class that dominated their historic capital, Tiflis (Tbilisi), and developed a way of life alien to the villagers. To the east, in and around Baku, the peasantry was almost entirely Azerbaijani, and urban society was stratified roughly along ethnic and religious lines, with Muslim workers at the bottom, Armenian and Russian workers in the more skilled positions, and Christian and European industrialists and capitalists dominating the oil industry.[2] Whereas ethnicity conferred social privilege on some and disadvantages on others, thus reinforcing differential social positions, vertical linguistic, cultural, and religious ties that united different social strata in a single "ethnic" community affected the horizontal class links in complex ways.

Though sometimes ethnicity reinforced class and vice versa, at other times ethnic loyalties cut across class lines and prevented horizontal solidarities. Muslim workers in the Baku region, for example, were separated from the more skilled Armenian workers, not only by wage differentials and class cultures, but also by their memories of the "Armenian-Tatar War" of 1905.[3] The bonds of religion and custom tied the Muslim workers to their Muslim compatriots, even to a Muslim capitalist. Both Muslim workers at the bottom of the labor hierarchy and Muslim industrialists near the top experienced condescension, not only from Russian officials and foreign capitalists, but also from Armenian entrepreneurs, engineers, and skilled workers.[4] In colonial Transcaucasia, the tsarist regime treated Christian Armenians more favorably than Muslims, and both Russians and Armenians, even sympathetic Social Democrats, viewed the Muslims as *temnye liudi*, unenlightened "dark people."

Which ties, ethnic or class, bound most tightly were contingent on the particular political and economic conjuncture and the intervention of intellectuals and activists. In moments of economic stress, in 1905, 1914, and 1917, workers of all ethnicities joined in broad strike movements and common political endeavors, with Russians active earlier and more enthusiastically than Armenians and Muslims. The links between them were always fragile and provisional, and by early 1918 ethnosocial fractures overwhelmed the best efforts of the Marxists and exploded in a new round of Armeno-Azerbaijani violence.

The peculiarities of Russian imperialism, still inadequately explored in both Western and Soviet scholarship, had a highly differentiated influence on the development of nationalities within the empire. Different forms of rule and the uneven effects of the socioeconomic transformations in Russia in the decades following the Emancipation of 1861 placed the various peoples of the empire in distinct historical contexts. The largest contiguous land empire in the world, Russia was content for much of its history to rule its *inorodtsy* and *inozemtsy* (the terms used for many of the non-Russian peoples; literally, people of other stock and other lands) in a mixed, contradictory system that involved indirect rule in some places, direct military government through local elites assimilated into the Russian administrative system in others, and various forms of constitutionalism (in the Grand Duchy of Finland and the Kingdom of Poland). For the Grand Dukes of Muscovy and the early tsars, empire-building was merely the extension of the tsar's sovereignty, through the institutions of his household and court, over the adjacent borderlands. "Neither Muscovites nor others were conscious of nationality in any sense that comes close to our modern sense," writes Marc Raeff, and expansion did not take ethnic distinctions into consideration.[5] The "gathering of Russian lands" meant, at different times, absorbing territories populated by Great Russians, the Volga regions held by the Kazan Tatars, and the Baltic littoral settled by Finnic peoples, Germans, and others. Peter the Great referred to his empire as *rossiiskaia* (of Russia) rather than with the ethnic term *russkaia*; the emperor, like his predecessors, paid little attention to the uniqueness or juridicial separateness of the conquered territories.

Russian imperialism was not driven by religious messianism; rather, its goal was state-building and security, seen by its practitioners as essentially defensive forays into an open environment where sparse but dangerous populations, often nomadic, threatened Russia's borders, Russian settlers, and commerce.[6] The "civilizing mission" of Russian expansion was intertwined with calculations of economic advantage. In the 1820s, tsarist officials debated the nature of its "colonial" relationship with newly acquired Transcaucasia. Foreign Minister Karl Nesselrode favored developing Tiflis as a center of trade with the Middle East, whereas Minister of Finance Egor Kankrin argued that

> the Transcaucasian provinces not without reason could be termed our colony, which should bring the state rather significant profits from the products of southern climes. . . . Calling the Transcaucasian territory a colony means that it is not the object of the government to join it to the general state system, that it is not hoped to make of this part of Russia and the Russian people in the moral sense, but to leave this territory as an Asian province, although better governed.[7]

With conquest came a program of coopting the local elites into the Russian administration and bringing native laws and economic procedures in line with general Russian practices.[8] Some native elites were more favored than others, notably the Slavic nobilities of the West, the Baltic Germans, and the Georgian *aznauroba* (nobility). But after the integration of the Tatar nobility into the Russian *dvorianstvo* (nobility) in the sixteenth century, only a few Muslim notables were able to retain their privileged status.[9]

Nationality was not a significant consideration for the Russian imperial state-builders. Religion and notions of inferior forms of social life were far more relevant. Jews were distinguished in the law as *inorodtsy*, indigenous ethnicities with special legal status or administration, and were lumped together with the nomadic Kalmyks and Kyrgyz (Kazakhs), the Samoeds, and the native peoples of Siberia.[10] Even here, the plasticity of ethnicity was clear, for assimilation was possible through self-Russification—more specifically, through conversion to orthodoxy.

Tsarism imposed a new state order—new regulations, taxation, and laws, and the imposition of serfdom in certain regions, such as Georgia—on societies that had had little contact with strong state structures. Its policy was to impose as much as possible a uniform way of life on all the tsar's subjects. But tsarism was anything but consistent. In contrast to this practice of "administrative Russification," the regime was at times extraordinarily tolerant of differences. Catherine the Great's policy toward Muslims, Alexander I's concessions to Finnish and Polish autonomy, and Viceroy Mikhail Vorontsov's recognition of local laws and customs in the Caucasus stand in stark contrast to Alexander II's attempts to convert Muslims, Alexander III's overt anti-Semitism, and Nicholas II's attack on Finnish privileges.[11] The administrative Russification involved in the extension of bureaucratic absolutism and the spontaneous self-Russification that non-Russians found advantageous in the first two-thirds of the nineteenth century were replaced after 1881 by an intermittent policy of forced cultural homogenization.[12]

Tsarist Russia had no "nationality policy," yet it legislated and operated with an ever-present awareness of ethnic and religious distinctions. In general, tsarist officials considered Belorussians and Ukrainians to be part of a greater Russian nation and forcefully discouraged the use of the Slavic languages of the western provinces. In 1863, Minister of the Interior Valuev declared that "a special Little Russian language [Ukrainian] has not existed, does not exist, and cannot exist." Thirteen years later, all printing and even performances in Ukrainian were forbidden. Not until 1905 was a Ukrainian Bible legally permitted.

Though confronted by a compact population of tens of millions of Poles in the formerly abolished Kingdom of Poland (1815–31), the government suppressed education in the Polish language, turned Warsaw University into an institution of Russification, restricted Polish ownership of land, and even forced shopkeepers to hang signs with Russian above or larger than the Polish. Driven from education and employment in the bureaucracy, Poles, like the Jews, faced lives of permanent disability. No matter how loyal they might in fact be, the regime regarded them—and, after 1881, most non-Russians—as alien and suspicious. Ethnicity carried with it not only marks of inferiority, but ascriptions of essential, indelible characteristics that conspired in the general discourse of ethnic stereotyping to hobble advancement in a discriminatory society and to drive many of the frustrated into active opposition.[13]

In the Russian empire, where the tsarist state promoted some peoples at some times (the Baltic Germans, the Armenian merchants until the 1880s) and discriminated against others (Jews, Ukrainians, Poles [particularly after 1863], Armenians after 1885, Finns at the turn of the century), the unequal relationships between ethnicities and the dominant, Russian nationality reinforced the sense of ethnic oppression and aspirations to national recognition. Especially after 1881, the ruling nationality increasingly conceived of social problems in ethnic terms and saw Jewish conspiracies, Armenian separatists, and nationalism in general as sources of disruption and rebellion. For Jews in particular, legally enforced demographic concentration in the Pale of Settlement and official racism that for all practical purposes prevented integration into Russian society preserved ethnocultural differences and determined the political strategies of Jewish activists.[14] Such discrimination against whole peoples, regardless of social status, eroded certain internal distinctions of members of the targeted ethnic group and engendered support for the conceptions of the nationalists. Yet even as the nationalist construction of the ethnic enemy gained in power, the economic policies of tsarism and considerations of security and profit prompted some national bourgeoisies to try to work with the Russifying regime.

Russian dominion in the Caucasus, Central Asia, and Siberia created a new degree of stability, a uniformity of laws, and slow but steady economic transformation. Whether this transformation was perceived as "progress" or the destruction of "traditional" societies, the effects proved to be irreversible. In the steppes of Central Asia, Russian land policy and immigration forced the nomadic Kazakhs to give up their seasonal migrations and settle as farmers. The very meaning of what it meant to be a Kazakh had to be rethought.[15] "To be a Kazakh," writes Martha Brill Olcott,

> was to be a nomad, as the Kazakh language suggests.
> Kazakh has terms for those who do not migrate, such as *balykhsh* (fisherman), *eginshi* (grain-grower), and the derogatory term *jatak* (literally lie-about), used to describe individuals who had lost their animals. . . . For the nomad and nomadism itself, Kazakh has no term.[16]

Identity here was linked more to a way of life than to a specific language group, more to "kinship" groups (themselves invented and mythically constructed) than to a universal religious community, such as Islam, or to abstract ideas of nation.

The breakdown of village isolation and the creation of links to the all-Russian market (through railroads) and to nearer trading towns blurred the distinction between kin and nonkin. At the same time, the state-driven industrialization in the last decade and a half of the nineteenth century gave rise to new forms of horizontal social cohesion among industrial workers, embattled industrialists and merchants, landlords and peasants, that were articulated by intellectuals borrowing from Western social thought. Russian social, economic, and intellectual developments in the post-Emancipation years paradoxically reinforced vertical ethnic ties in some cases and horizontal social bonds in others. The experience of peoples who continued to have little representation in towns (e.g., Lithuanians, Ukrainians, and Belorussians)—or, if they did migrate to industrial or urban centers, tended to assimilate with the predominately Russian work force—differed radically from the experiences of ethnicities (like the Georgians, Latvians, Estonians, Jews, and to an extent, Armenians) who were more directly affected by industrial capitalism, developed a working class of their own, and came into more immediate contact with the radical intelligentsia. Furthest removed from the social revolution of industrialism were the Muslim peoples of the empire. Though one must be careful to differentiate between those Muslim peoples, like the Azerbaijanis and the Volga Tatars, that had a significant if small urban presence, the vast majority of Central Asians, many of whom were nomadic or seminomadic, had relatively little urban experience and almost no contact with the socialist or nationalist intelligentsia. Yet even the lives of the most isolated villagers had been transformed by the imposition of bureaucratic administration, the development of domestic and international agricultural markets, and Russian migration.

As the seigneurial economy gave way to market relations and new forms of the exploitation of labor replaced more traditional and paternalistic ones, radical intellectuals articulated the sufferings of newly minted workers in the idiom of Marxism. But the interconnection of ethnic and social discontents made it difficult, even for those peoples who entered industrial and city life, to separate class from ethnic experience. The embryonic working classes of Russia's peripheries remained ambivalent about nationalism in most cases and expressed their political consciousnesses through ethnic socialist movements. Peasantries, though ethnically cohesive, were also generally indifferent to the nationalists' programs.

The discourses of class (socialism) and nationality (nationalism) were largely urban phenomena in prerevolutionary Russia. No matter how sincerely patriots extolled the virtues of the peasantry, making actual converts among villagers proved to be as difficult for the followers of the Ukrainian patriotic poet Taras Shevchenko as for the disciples of Marx. In part, this difficulty was the result of the perceptual limitations of those nationalists who tended to emphasize the unity of the "nation" and neglect social conflicts and divisions, and of those socialists who promoted class divisions and were dismissive of, if not hostile to, ethnic solidarities. Nationalists and socialists alike failed to appreciate the complex meshing of social and ethnic grievances in situations where class and ethnicity reinforced individual and collective positions in the hierarchy of power and powerlessness.

Socialism and Nationalism in the Revolution

Although most of the non-Russian peoples of the tsarist empire were overwhelmingly peasant, they differed radically from one another in their internal class structures and in the degrees of their national consciousness. It is useful to cluster nine major nationalities in the Russian empire at the time of the revolution—four Baltic peoples, three Transcaucasian peoples, and two Western Slavic peoples—into five subgroups, based on their identifications with class or nationality. The first group, distinguished by their almost completely peasant composition and low level of national consciousness, includes the Belorussians, Lithuanians, and Azerbaijanis. The second, marked by social and geographic divisions and a profound ambiguity in their national and class orientations, involves the Ukrainians and the Estonians. A third group, consisting of the Georgians and the Latvians, resolved the tension between nationality and class through socialist-oriented national movements. The fourth group—the Finns—divided into fiercely opposing camps, one socialist, the other nationalist, that resolved their conflict through bloody civil war. The Armenians, who comprise the fifth group, subordinated class divisions to a vertically integrating nationalism. This typology illustrates the variety of socially and ethnically generated responses to the new opportunities offered by the revolution.

Group I: Belorussians, Lithuanians, and Azerbaijanis

BELORUSSIANS Echoing the consensus among scholars, one investigator notes that "the Belorussians were predominantly a peasant people hardly touched by the consciousness of a unique national identity. The political cause of Belorussian nationalism commanded the barest following. . . . Socialism and assimilation into the Russian nation vied with Belorussian nationalism for the loyalties of the Belorussian people."[17] The Belorussian peasantry was the repository of the culture and languages of those eastern Slavs who had succumbed neither to Polish culture and language (as had much of the local nobility) nor to the Russian language and culture of the towns. Nearly three-quarters of the people of the Belorussian provinces were illiterate. They spoke up to twenty local dialects "differing from one another nearly as much as they differed, in one respect or another, from Russian, Polish, or Ukrainian."[18] Large estates dominated the countryside, whereas the towns and cities of the region were predominantly inhabited by Russians, Poles, and, most numerously, Jews. In 1897, Belorussian speakers made up only 9 percent of the inhabitants of Minsk, the city that eventually would be selected as the capital of the Belorussian Soviet Republic. Over 51 percent were Yiddish speakers, 25.5 percent Russian, and 11.4 percent Polish.

With very low literacy rates and less than 2 percent of Belorussian speakers living in towns over 2,000 inhabitants, the Belorussians had only a small national intellectual elite to articulate a vision of separate nationhood. With no literary tradition of their own, Belorussians were first recognized as a distinct ethnic group by scholars in the early nineteenth century, who distinguished the local idiom from Polish and Russian. A few poems in Belorussian vernacular appeared in the late eighteenth century, followed by a parody of the *Aeneid* in the Smolensk dialect. Not until 1918 was the first major grammar of Belorussian produced. "It is noteworthy," writes Nicholas Vakar,

> that neither the Polish nor the Russian side using the Belorussian vernacular identified it with Belorussian nationality. Nor was there any such concept among the Belorussians themselves. Literary activities fostering provincial patriotism centered around a thin layer of the educated gentry, divided into two camps. There is no historical evidence that they had any response from the masses. But the important fact was that the spoken idiom received recognition as a literary medium [in the mid-nineteenth century], and now was used as such by the very people who ignored it only a decade or two before. When, in 1867, the Government prohibited its use, the language gained new significance and moral strength.[19]

Social protest was not unknown among the local peasants. Many had participated in the uprisings of 1863, angered by the terms of the tsar's emancipation of the serfs and stimulated by the Polish rebellion. But a Belorussian ethnic nationalism found its voice only in the last decades of the nineteenth century, and even then as part of the broader discourse of the Russian revolutionary movement. Revolutionary populists formed a *Zemlia i volia* (Land and Liberty) circle in Minsk in the 1870s, and a small group of young revolutionaries in St. Petersburg, again allied to the Russian *narodniki* (populists), started up an illegal newspaper, *Homam* (Talk), in which they advocated an autonomous Belorussia within a Russian federation.[20] More impressively, in 1902, Belorussian students in the Russian capital, with the help of Polish socialists, founded the Belorussian Revolutionary *Hramada* (party or association). Renamed the Belorussian Socialist *Hramada* a year later, the party was made up of both social democratic and populist activists, and it proposed the formation of a Belorussian state as a first step toward the solution of social problems.

A small part of the radical Belorussian intelligentsia, those we might refer to as nationalists, did not find a contradiction between socialism and the struggle for national-cultural, even political, autonomy. These nationalists saw the distinctiveness of spoken Belorussian (which Russifying tsarist officials claimed to be merely a dialect of Russian) and its use in some literary and juridical works as proof of unique national development. Further, what was for their opponents an unnatural, centuries-old separation of one part of the eastern Slavic peoples from those of central Russia and Ukraine was for the nationalists the historical justification for their claims to autonomy.

The Belorussian provinces had not fallen under Mongol rule in the post-Kievan period, and were later incorporated into the Grand Duchy of Lithuania. In the late Middle Ages, the Slavic dialect of this area dominated this great state, and nationalists hold that the code of laws of 1529 was written in Belorussian. With the Union of Lublin in 1569, Belorussia and Lithuania were linked to Poland, and cultural, religious, and linguistic influences from the Catholic rulers of the new state were reflected in the social hierarchy, in which a Polonized nobility ruled over peasants who spoke Lithuanian or Belorussian. For later Belorussian nationalists, language, rather than religion, was the touchstone of nationality, because Belorussians were divided between an Orthodox majority and a Catholic minority.

The nationalists were never very influential in the multiethnic towns, nor among the mass of peasants primarily concerned with local social problems. The peasants made little distinction between a generalized "Russian" culture and a specifically Belorussian nationality.[21] The closeness of the Belorussian language to Russian and other Slavic languages of the area permitted easy access to related cultures and blurred ethnic boundaries.

With the collapse of tsarism, the weakness of the nationalists and relative strength of non-nationalist socialists, most notably the Bolsheviks, became more evident. All-Russian and Jewish parties dominated the political scene in Minsk, and the Belorussian National Committee fell under the influence of the Socialist Revolutionary Party (SRs). In the battle of committees and congresses that often characterized revolutionary politics, Bolsheviks held sway in the local peasant congress, electing as chairman one of their military leaders, Mikhail Frunze. The National Committee denounced the congress as a "Russifying tendency."[22] The nationalists, influenced by local SRs, formed a *Rada* (council) in July, adopted a program of agrarian reform directed against the landlords, and promoted the formation of Belorussian military units.

The progress of the revolution in Belorussia was fundamentally influenced by the Russo-German battle lines that ran through the region. Russian soldiers, increasingly influenced by Bolshevism, played a key role in the formation of the first soviets and the establishment of a Soviet government in Minsk just after the October Revolution. The Armenian Bolshevik Aleksandr Miasnikov was appointed chairman of a Military-Revolutionary Committee (*Revkom*), which was immediately opposed by a "Committee to Save the Revolution and Fatherland" made up of SRs and Mensheviks and supported by the nationalists. The peasants remained outside the political struggle in the towns and gave little encouragement to either the socialists or the nationalists. In the elections to the Constituent Assembly in November, the Bolsheviks secured over 60 percent of the vote (in large part thanks to soldiers), whereas the *Hramada* failed to elect a single delegate.[23]

As winter approached, the uneven struggle in the towns pitted the nationalists and moderate socialists around the *Rada* against the Bolsheviks, with their supporters in the Russian Army. Despite their lack of popular support, the *Hramada* called a Belorussian National Congress in December. Broadly representative of the politically active population, particularly the military, the congress was at first tolerated by the Bolsheviks. It recognized Soviet power in the center but not the local Council of People's Commissars of the Western Region. When on December 17–18 the congress declared Belorussia independent, the Bolsheviks used their military muscle to disperse the delegates.

Soviet power remained in Belorussia until the Brest-Litovsk Treaty forced the Russians to retreat, and the Germans backed the nationalists' declaration of independence (March 25, 1918).[24] The Germans dismissed the more socialist nationalists from the new government and promoted more conservative nationalists. The peasants, who had been taking what land they could since late 1917, resisted the German occupation and gravitated toward the Communists. Shortly after the German withdrawal in December and the entry of the army of the Russian Soviet Republic into Minsk, the Central Committee of the Russian Communist Party (Bolsheviks) (RKP[b]) decided to form a distinct Communist Party of Belorussia and to establish a Belorussian Soviet Socialist Republic (BSSR). In February 1919, the First All-Belorussian Congress of Soviets proclaimed first the BSSR, and shortly after a joint Lithuanian-Belorussian Soviet Republic, soon to be known as Litbel. Belorussia once again became the battleground on which the border between Poland and the Soviet republics would be decided, and only on August 1, 1920, were the Communists able to reestablish a Soviet republic in the part of Belorussia they held.

In Belorussia, one may conclude, national awareness came late, remained an intellectual phenomenon, and did not take hold among the peasants. A national state was created, first by nationalist intellectuals, and later by the Communists in the anti-German and anti-Polish campaigns. During the years of revolution and civil war, the nationalist "movement," if it can be called that, was almost always "a pawn in the larger schemes of the German military, Polish nationalists, and Russian revolutionists."[25] Nicholas Vakar in his study of Belorussian nationhood writes:

> It has been said that nationhood came to the Belorussians as an almost unsolicited gift of the Russian Revolution. It was, in fact, received from the hands of the Austro-German Occupation Army authorities and depended on their good will. The Belorussian National Republic held no general elections, and the self-appointed administration lacked the elements necessary for international recognition. It may have been well-meaning, but it had neither the power nor the time to make reforms effective. Furthermore, its subservience to the Central Powers alienated many loyal elements in the population.[26]

LITHUANIANS   In Lithuania, a number of factors inhibited the development of a broad-based nationalism. Like their neighbors, the Belorussians, Lithuanians had no urban presence to speak of, and nationalist sentiments did not reach much beyond the relatively insignificant intelligentsia and the large Lithuanian diaspora. The upper class in the region was Polonized, and the Lithuanian peasantry was mixed with Belorussian speakers (who made up 56 percent of Vilnius [Wilno in Polish, Vilna in Russian] province). Towns were either Jewish or Polish in culture; Vilnius was 40 percent Jewish, 31 percent Polish. Yet here the very differentness of the Lithuanian language from the neighboring Slavic tongues kept Lithuanian-speaking peasants separate from others with whom they shared a socioeconomic position.

Lithuanians speak an Indo-European language (classified along with Latvian as Eastern Baltic) and have been present in the Baltic region since classical times. Lithuanian tribes united briefly in the thirteenth century to resist German incursions, but the great medieval state around Vilnius was a multiethnic commonwealth that used Belorussian, and later Latin, in its official communications. In the first half of the nineteenth century, some Polish and German intellectuals and clergymen began collecting and publishing Lithuanian folk songs and popular art, but only in the 1870s did Lithuanian students begin to distance themselves from Polish culture. Three literary languages competed for recognition (so-called Low, East High, and West High Lithuanian) until Jonas Jablonskis succeeded in establishing his own dialect (closest to West High Lithuanian) as the modern standard.

Miroslav Hroch argues that intellectuals of peasant background were quite important in Lithuania in the absence of a national bourgeoisie, and that the nationalist agitation had no effect on the towns. Even the Church did not support a separate Lithuanian identity, but encouraged ties to Poland and antagonism to Russia.[27] Before 1905, the tsarist authorities allowed only one newspaper in Lithuanian to be published, the official gazette *Dabertis*; other periodicals, like *Ausra* (Dawn, 1883–86) and *Varpas* (Bell, 1889–1904), had to be smuggled from abroad.

With Lithuania occupied by the Germans through much of the early revolutionary period, the first free political expressions occurred among Lithuanians in Petrograd. At a congress of Lithuanians held in the Russian capital in early June, nationalists passed a resolution in favor of Lithuanian independence, but the center and left, unwilling to antagonize "democratic Russia," called instead for a recognition of Lithuania's right to self-determination.[28] On the other hand, the creation of a Lithuanian National Council, the *Taryba*, in September 1917 and the declaration of independence in December were both carried out under German supervision. The nationalists, led by Antanas Smetona among others, antagonized local Poles by rejecting any form of union or federation with an independent Poland.

As in many other regions in the western borderlands, the creation of independent Lithuania was not the result of a broad-based and coherent nationalist movement that realized long-held aspirations to nationhood. Rather, it was the artificial result of German politics and the immediate weakness of the central Russian state. Here "nationality" was the instrument that a Great Power used to destroy the Russian empire and create mini-states it could control, as elsewhere and at other times "class" would be the basis on which the Soviets would reconstruct a multinational state.

Through the years of the Russian Civil War, Lithuanian lands were contested by the nationalists whom the Germans had patronized, the Communists backed by the Red Army, and the independent Poles under Josef Pilsudski. When the Germans evacuated Vilnius at the end of the World War, a Communist government was installed by the Red Army. In April 1919, the Poles took Vilnius, and the nationalists, installed in their new capital of Kaunas, used the Soviet-Polish antagonism to secure Moscow's recognition of their independence. Only with the conclusion of the Russo-Polish War in 1920 and intricate negotiations through the League of

Nations were firm borders established between a reduced Lithuania, a Soviet state pushed eastward, and a bloated Poland that included Vilnius as well as Ukrainian and Belorussian territories.

AZERBAIJANIS   In the course of the nineteenth century, three related processes—the imposition of tsarist rule, the rise of the market and capitalist relations of production, and the emergence of secular national intelligentsias—initiated a long transformation of the ethnoreligious communities of Transcaucasia into more politically conscious and mobilized nationalities. The social and political evolutions of these communities, though distinct, were deeply influenced by the trajectories of the other peoples of the Caucasus. Tsarism eliminated barriers between Georgian principalities, brought Armenians of Russia and the former Persian provinces under a single legal order, and imposed uniform laws and taxation systems on the Muslims of Transcaucasia. Imperial rule brought relative peace and security, the fostering of commerce and industry, the growth of towns, the building of railroads, and the slow end to the isolation of many villages. At the same time, the imposition of bureaucratic absolutism on the looser political structures of Transcaucasia and the initial undermining of local elites gave rise to resistance by both the gentry (as in the Georgian noble conspiracy of 1831) and the peasants. By mid-century, a more accommodating tsarism, represented by the effective administration of Viceroy Mikhail Vorontsov, drew both Muslim and Georgian landlords into the Russian *dvorianstvo* (nobility) and employed them as local governors.

The three major peoples of Transcaucasia developed unevenly and at different rates. Armenians were the most urban, Azerbaijanis the least. Georgians and Azerbaijanis were the most compact populations, living in coherent territories, whereas Armenians were dispersed. Clerics dominated Azerbaijani society; the old national mobility held sway among Georgians; and a merchant middle class was the most important social group among the Armenians. Though intellectuals of all three peoples were deeply influenced by the debates in Russia and shared appreciation for the insights of Western Marxists, the leading Armenian, Azerbaijani, and Georgian intellectuals and politicians developed disparate discourses that ultimately distanced each of them from the others.

The demographically dominant people in eastern Transcaucasia were known in the nineteenth century as "Tatars," but by the late 1930s the ethnym "Azerbaijani" (*azarbayjanli*), favored by the national leaders, was universally adopted.[29] In ancient and early medieval times, eastern Transcaucasia was populated by Iranian speakers, some nomadic Turkic tribes, and the Caucasian Albanians, a little-known people who converted to Christianity in the fourth century and came under the cultural influence of the Armenians. After Arab incursions in the seventh century, Islamic polities were established under local rulers called *Shahvanshah*. The Seljuk invasions in the eleventh century changed the composition of the local population and resulted in the linguistic dominance of Oghuz Turkic dialects. But unlike the Ottoman Turks who came to dominate Anatolia, the Caucasian Muslims of Azerbaijan in the early sixteenth century became Shi'i rather than Sunni Muslims, and continued to develop under Persian social and cultural influence. No specifically Azerbaijani state existed before 1918, and rather than imagining themselves as part of a continuous national tradition, like the Georgians and Armenians, the Muslims of Transcaucasia saw themselves as part of the larger Muslim world, the *'umma*.

Annexation to the Russian empire in a series of wars separated the Azerbaijani Turks of Caucasia from their linguistic and religious compatriots in Iran. Azerbaijanis in both Iran and Russia remained a largely extraurban population, though small merchant and working classes grew up on both sides of the border. As Baku became the major source of oil for Russia, tens of thousands of Iranian workers streamed to the Apsheron peninsula in search of employment, and Russian economic and political influence could be felt in both parts of Azerbaijan. As the main source of employment and the home of the nascent Azerbaijani intelligentsia and revolutionary movement, Baku radiated its influence in Iranian Azerbaijan as well as north of the Arax River border.

The migrant Muslim villagers, whom members of educated society often considered to be an unenlightened, benighted people, found themselves in a town dominated by Russians and Armenians. Baku, which until the turn of the century produced as much oil as the whole of the United States, was segregated, with Russians and Armenians in the central part of the town and Muslims clustered in distinct outer districts. Social resentments festered, particularly in times of political uncertainty, and ethnoreligious differences, enhanced by feelings of inferiority and superiority, defined the battle lines in bloody clashes between Azerbaijanis and local Armenians in 1905 and 1918.

Within the working class, a hierarchy of skills, education, and wages began with Muslims (both local Muslims and those who migrated from Persia to work in the oil fields) on the bottom, Armenians and Russians in the middle, and local Christians and Europeans at the top. Social status and ethnicity overlapped in complex ways. Nationality reinforced class, and vice versa. Poor Muslim workers developed resentments against skilled workers and employers, most of whom were Christians. Armenians and Russians were either blind to the concerns of Muslims or condescending in their behavior. By virtue of property holdings and a legal quota on Muslim representation, the Baku city *duma* remained in the hands of wealthy Armenians and Russians.[30]

Incorporation into the Russian empire provided a new

outlet for educated Azerbaijanis, some of whom turned from their religious upbringings to a more secular outlook.[31] Low literacy, inadequate schooling, and poverty among Azerbaijanis slowed the development of a Turkic intelligentsia, but individuals, often with Russian education, flirted with the intellectual trends of the time: socialism, liberalism, Pan-Turkism, Pan-Islam. The more radical joined the Russian socialist movement. No single, coherent ideology or movement dominated Azerbaijani intellectuals, though by 1905 a growing number had adopted the program of 'Ali bay Huseynzada: "Turkify, Islamicize, Europeanize" (*Turklashtirmak, Islamlashtirmak, Avrupalashtirmak*).

The center of Azerbaijani intellectual and political life, Baku, was not a city that Muslims controlled in any sense; rather, it was a dynamic multinational city in which a powerful labor movement challenged the oil industrialists' hold over the population. Led by Russians and working closely with Marxist intellectuals, the workers won significant concessions from the owners, including the first general labor contract in the Russian empire in 1904. Azerbaijanis themselves remained on the fringe of the labor movement, indifferent to or ignorant of the aspirations of both socialist and nationalist intellectuals. None of the small parties and political groups that arose after 1905 commanded much of a following beyond the intelligentsia. At the same time, however, anxiety about the Armenian "threat," distance from and hostility to this privileged element within their midst, and a feeling of connection to other Muslims, particularly Turks, became part of an Azerbaijani sense of self.

Though Azerbaijani political activists participated in the revival of Muslim organizations in the first year of the revolution, traveling to congresses and issuing manifestos, in Baku the political center was held by Russian Social Democrats (SDs) and Armenian nationalists, the *Dashnaktsutiun* (Armenian Revolutionary Federation) in particular. The Azerbaijanis identified Soviet power in 1917–18 with the Christians, and in March 1918, the city soviet in Baku put down a revolt by Muslims with the help of Armenian nationalists. Soviet power met indifference or active resistance when it attempted to extend its sway over the surrounding countryside and the Azerbaijani town of Gandja (Elisavetpol').

The Baku Commune, a Soviet government that ruled Baku from April to late July 1918, failed in its attempt to rally the peoples of Transcaucasia around Soviet power. After crushing a Muslim revolt in the city, the Bolshevik-led government, with its small Red Guard, was forced to rely on Armenian troops led by Dashnak officers. Though the Azerbaijani nationalist leaders, located in Gandja, had been largely pro-Russian in the prewar years, they welcomed the leverage and support offered by the advancing Ottoman Turkish army, and they entered Baku with those troops. In September 1918, Azerbaijanis took their revenge for the "March Days," killing between nine and thirty thousand local Armenians.

But even as they secured control over the city that was to become their capital, the Azerbaijani nationalists faced a mixed population of Russian, Armenian, and Muslim workers who had undergone a long socialist and trade unionist education. Never fully secure in Baku, where Bolshevism had deep roots, the nationalists relied on foreigners, first the Turks and later the British, to back them against the Reds. Among the peasantry whom they claimed to represent, national consciousness was still largely absent. When the Red Army marched into Baku in April 1920, there was little resistance. As Tadeusz Swietochowski writes in a recent study of Azerbaijani national identity:

> While the intelligentsia experienced an evolution that took it in quick succession from Pan-Islamism to Turkism to Azerbaijanism, the masses remained on the level of 'umma consciousness with its typical indifference to secular power, foreign or native. The idea of an Azerbaijani nation-state did not take root among the majority of the population; the very term *nationalism* was

either not understood by them or, worse, it rang with the sound of a term of abuse, a fact the Communists exploited in their propaganda against the Azerbaijani Republic. This might help explain why the overthrow of the republic was amazingly easy. Even those who subsequently rebelled against Soviet rule did not fight for the restoration of the fallen regime.[32]

Unlike the Armenians and Georgians, Azerbaijanis did not create a mass political movement under an effective leadership until well after the revolution and civil war.

Group II: Ukrainians and Estonians

UKRAINIANS A far more complex and ambiguous relationship between nationality and other social identities existed among the Ukrainians and Estonians, in whom national consciousness was more developed than in the nationalities of Group I, though not strong or widespread enough to overwhelm competing identities.

Scholars agree that in Ukraine nationality coincided to an unusual degree with economic class. Except for a small intelligentsia, Ukrainians were almost entirely peasants; the landowners and officials were Poles or Russians, whereas the commercial bourgeoisie was largely Jewish.[33] Steven L. Guthier writes:

> Class and ethnic cleavages were closely related. . . . Russians manned the oppressive bureaucracy and were heavily represented among the principal landowners. Poles dominated the *pomeshchiki* class in the right bank provinces of Kiev, Podolia, and Volhynia. Petty trade, commerce, and much of industry on the right bank were controlled by Jews who were therefore the peasantry's most visible creditors. As a consequence, the ethnic and socioeconomic grievances of the Ukrainian peasant proved mutually reinforcing and provided the foundation for a political movement which combined nationalism with a populist social program.[34]

Ukraine had developed a distinct ethnic culture and language in the long period from the fall of Kiev to the Mongols (1240) through the Polish dominion (1569) to the union with Russia (1654). Early in the nineteenth century, nationalist intellectuals articulated a notion of Ukrainian distinctiveness, and the Romantics Taras Shevchenko and Panko Kulish formed a Ukrainian literary language from the vernacular of the southeast.[35] The brief flourishing of Eastern Ukrainian intellectual culture in the first two-thirds of the nineteenth century was curtailed after the Polish insurrection of 1863, however, particularly in 1876, when the tsarist state prohibited public expression in Ukrainian. With the restrictions on "Russian" Ukrainian culture, Galicia, which contained the Western Ukrainian regions under Austrian rule, became the center for literary expression and a popular nationalism.[36] In contrast, "Russian" Ukraine, a vast territory with non-Ukrainians dominating urban centers and state-imposed constraints on ethnic intellectual life, developed neither a coherent mass-based national movement nor even a widely shared sense of a Ukrainian nation in the decades before the twentieth-century revolutions.

Ukrainian peasants were very active in 1905–7, though the movement in the first revolution had only superficially nationalistic characteristics. Largely a protest over land shortages, which were blamed on the large holdings by noble landlords (most of them Polish and Russian), social discontent led to violence, but with minimal ethnic expression. Even the supposedly traditional Ukrainian anti-Semitism was largely absent, and Jewish revolutionaries were welcomed as supporters of the peasant movement.[37] Peasant grievances were sufficient to generate protests without consistent intervention from outsiders, though "*Spilka*" (the Ukrainian Social Democratic Union) was active on the right bank, and the SRs and the Peasants' Union were active on the left bank.[38]

Historians differ in their evaluations of Ukrainian nationalism in 1917–18. Without question, an articulate and active nationalist elite, made up of middle-class professionals, was prepared to confront both the Provisional Government

(March–October 1917) and the *Sovnarkom* (Lenin's Council of People's Commissars) with its demand for autonomy and self-rule.[39] John Reshetar, the author of the first major scholarly monograph on the Ukrainian Revolution, writes:

> Immediately after the March Revolution, leadership in the Ukrainian national movement was assumed by the democratically inclined petite bourgeoisie, the intelligentsia with nationalist sympathies, and the middle strata of the peasantry which supported the cooperative movement. The peasant masses, the soldiers, and the urban proletariat were not participants at this early period, and it cannot be said that the national movement permeated their ranks to any significant extent in the months that followed since it was competing with more urgent social and economic issues.[40]

The *Rada* was committed to finding a democratic solution to the political crisis, to remaining within a federated Russian state, and to launching a radical program of land reform. Its support in the cities was minimal. In the elections in July to the municipal *duma* in Kiev, Ukrainian parties won only 20 percent of the vote, whereas Russian parties garnered 67 percent (Russian socialists, 37 percent; "Russian voters," 15 percent; Kadets, 9 percent; Bolsheviks, 6 percent), but the Ukrainian politicians were backed by Ukrainian soldiers, who were particularly interested in the formation of ethnic military units.[41]

Far more problematic, however, is the estimate of the level of national cohesion among Ukrainians and the degree of support for the national program among the peasants. For Reshetar, nationalism is a middle-class movement and the peasant "was enslaved by his locale and regarded the inhabitants of the neighboring villages as a species of foreigner." The absence of a Ukrainian bourgeoisie of any weight and the

> essentially agrarian character of late nineteenth-century Ukrainian society, with its emphasis on the locale, tended to retard the development of that sentiment of group cohesiveness which transcends localism and is termed national consciousness. The

peasant, because of his conservatism, was able to retain his language, peculiarities of dress, and local customs despite foreign rule, but initially he resisted the notion that all Ukrainians, whether living in Kharkiv [Kharkov] province, in Volynia, or in Carpatho-Ukraine, belonged to the same nation.

Though this peasant parochialism was partially broken down by the spread of a money economy, the building of railroads, and the dissemination of newspapers and periodicals, the protracted process of nationality formation "had not been consummated as late as 1917." Reshetar points out that even in 1917, peasants in Ukraine referred to themselves not as a single collective but with regional terms: Rusins (sons of Rus), Galicians, Bukovinians, Uhro-rusins, Lemkos, and Hutsuls. Russophilia was still strong in many parts of the country, even among the peasantry, and the middle and working classes were largely Russified.[42]

In his encyclopedic study of nationalism in the revolutionary years, a work sympathetic to the aspirations of the nationalists and repelled by the opportunism and centralism of the Bolsheviks, Richard Pipes repeatedly demonstrates that social environment—the isolation of the nationalists from urban society and the working class, and their dependency on and difficulties in mobilizing the peasantry—confounded the plans of the Ukrainian ethnic parties.[43] Agreeing with Reshetar that "the weakest feature of the Ukrainian national movement was its dependence on the politically disorganized, ineffective, and unreliable village," Pipes emphasizes the village's "political immaturity, which made [it] easily swayed by propaganda, and . . . strong inclinations toward anarchism." Nevertheless, for Pipes, nationalism was a reality in Ukraine, "a political expression of genuine interests and loyalties," which had its roots in

a specific Ukrainian culture, resting on peculiarities of language and folklore; a historic tradition dating from the seventeenth-century Cossack communities; an identity of interests among the members of the large and powerful group of well-to-do peasants of the Dnieper region; and a numerically small but active group of nationally conscious intellectuals, with a century-old heritage of cultural nationalism behind them.

But "the fate of the Ukraine, as of the remainder of the Empire, was decided in the towns, where the population was almost entirely Russian in its culture, and hostile to Ukrainian nationalism."[44] Contingent factors, such as the inexperience of the national leaders and the shortage of administrative personnel, are mentioned as part of the toxic mix that destroyed the Ukrainian experiment in independence. Pipes takes nationalism as a natural and admirable development, whereas he sees communism as an artificial implant forcibly imposed upon non-Russians.

Though one might hesitate to accept Reshetar's firm requirement that a middle class must exist for a nationalist movement to succeed, or Pipes's assumption that there was a conscious community of interests between intelligentsia and peasantry in 1917, the argument that the movement would stand or fall on the backs of the peasantry seems compelling. In a most intriguing article, Steven L. Guthier argues, in contrast to Reshetar, that the Ukrainian peasantry was nationally conscious in 1917, as demonstrated in the November elections to the Constituent Assembly, in which the peasantry overwhelmingly supported Ukrainian parties. In the eight Ukrainian provinces (Kiev, Poltava, Podolia, Volhynia, Ekaterinoslav, Chernigov, Kherson, and Kharkov), "55 percent of all votes cast outside the Ukraine's ten largest cities went to lists dominated by the UPSR [Ukrainian Party of Socialist Revolutionaries] and 'Selians'ska Spilka' [All-Ukrainian Peasants' Union]; another 16 percent went to Left PSR/UPSR slates."[45] The cities, on the other hand, went for Russian and Jewish parties, though a heavy turnout of Ukrainian soldiers gave substantial backing to Ukrainian parties.

Guthier concludes that "Ukrainian nationalism as a substantial political force was a one-class movement," but one in which identification between peasant aspirations and the programs of the national parties was quite close.[46] He assumes that peasants voting for the Ukrainian peasant parties were aware of and accepted the national planks in their programs. "The peasants were committed to the creation of a Ukraine which was both autonomous and socialist. They wanted land rights to be reserved for those who farmed the land with their own hands."[47]

A useful distinction might be made, however, between cultural or ethnic awareness and full-blown political nationalism—that is, an active commitment to realizing a national agenda. Although the 1917 election results show that peasants in Ukraine preferred parties and leaders of their own ethnicity, people who could speak to them in their own language and promised to secure their local interests, these results do not provide sufficient evidence either that the peasantry conceived of itself as a single nationality or that it could be effectively mobilized to defend ideals of national autonomy or independence. Though the mentality of the Ukrainian peasants in 1917 needs to be explored further, they seem to have been ethnically aware, preferring their own kind to strangers, but not yet moved by a passion for the nation, and certainly not willing to sacrifice their lives for anything beyond the village. Defeated nationalists, as well as "class-conscious" Bolsheviks, considered the peasants of Ukraine to be "backward," "unconscious," unable to be mobilized except for the most destructive, anarchistic ends. But one might more generously argue that rather than being backward, Ukrainian peasants had their own localistic agenda in the chaos of the civil war, one that did not mesh neatly either with that of urban intellectuals, nationalist or Bolshevik, or with that of workers, many of whom despised those living in the villages.

Guthier may be closer to the mark when he sees the momentary coincidence of peasant voters and Ukrainian populists as the specific conjuncture when "national autonomy was seen as the best guarantee that the socioeconomic reconstruction of the Ukraine would reflect local, not all-Russian conditions."[48] Here once again both the contingent and evolving character of nationalism (and class, for that matter) and the closeness of ethnic and social factors become clear. At least in 1917–18, the Ukrainian peasants were most concerned about the agrarian question and their own suffering in the years of war and scarcity.[49] They thought of themselves as peasants, which for them was the same as being "Ukrainian" (or whatever they might have called themselves locally). Their principal hope was for agrarian reform and the end of the oppression identified with the state and the city. Russians, Jews, and Poles were the sources of that oppression, and it is conceivable that for many peasants the promise of autonomy was seen as the means to achieving the end to the onerous and arbitrary power of those groups. But ethnic claims had no priority over social ones in these early years of revolution, and alliances with nationalists (or, more frequently, with ethnic populists) could easily be replaced by marriages of convenience with more radical elements.[50]

When the nationalist *Rada* was unable to resist effectively the Bolshevik advance in January 1918, it turned as a last resort to the Germans, who requisitioned grain and terrorized peasants. When the nationalists failed to back up their own agrarian reform, support rapidly evaporated. As a consequence of the German occupation, the nationalist forces in Ukraine splintered into competing groups. The nationalist cause was identified by many as linked to foreign intervention; to antinationalist elements, particularly in towns, the only viable alternative to social chaos, foreign dependence, and Ukrainian chauvinism appeared to be the Bolsheviks. A German report of March 1918 gives a sense of the fragmentation in Ukraine at the time, the uncertainty of nationalist influence, and the relative strength of the Bolsheviks:

> It is not true that the Bolsheviks are supported only by the Russian soldiers who remained in the Ukraine. . . . They have a large following in the country. All the industrial workers are with them, as is also a considerable part of the demobilized soldiers. The attitude of the peasants, however, is very difficult to ascertain. The villages that have once been visited by Bolshevik gangs . . . are, as a rule, anti-Bolshevik. In other places Bolshevik propaganda seems to be successful among the peasants.
>
> The peasants are concerned chiefly with the dividing up of the land; they will follow the Rada if it allows them to take the estates of the landlords . . . as proclaimed in the Third and Fourth Universals. . . . Otherwise they will go with the Bolsheviks. Although the Bolsheviks lost out in many places because of their system of terror, their slogan "Take everything, all is yours" is too attractive and tempting to the masses.
>
> The Ukrainian separatist movement, on which the Rada is relying, has no true roots in the country and is supported only by a small group of political dreamers. The people as a whole show complete indifference to national self-determination.[51]

Sadly for the nationalists and happily for the Bolsheviks, the peasantry proved to be an unsteady social base for a political movement. A British observer in May 1918 confirmed to the Foreign Office the lack of national consciousness among the Ukrainian peasants.

> The peasants speak the Little Russian dialect; a small group of nationalist *intelligentsia* now professes an Ukrainian nationality distinct from that of the Great Russians. Whether such a nationality exists is usually discussed in terms in which the question can receive no answer. Were one to ask the average peasant in the Ukraine his nationality he would answer that he is Greek Orthodox; if pressed to say whether he is a Great Russian, a Pole, or an Ukrainian, he would probably reply that he is a peasant; and if one insisted on knowing what language he spoke, he would say that he talked "the local tongue." One might perhaps get him to call himself by a proper national name and say that he is "russki," but this declaration would hardly yet prejudge the question of an Ukrainian relationship; he simply does not think of nationality in the terms familiar to the *intel-*

ligentsia. Again, if one tried to find out to what State he desires to belong—whether he wants to be ruled by an All-Russian or a separate Ukrainian Government—one would find that in his opinion all Governments alike are a nuisance, and that it would be best if the "Christian peasant-folk" were left to themselves.[52]

When the Directory, which came to power in November 1918 and tried to place itself at the head of the peasant risings against the Hetmanate,

> faltered in its implementation of new programs, turning cautious and conservative in order to preserve its very life, the forces of the Jacquerie swept past it to embrace another, more radical political group, which seemed to promise a program that *would* suit peasant tastes. Specifically, even before the year 1918 had run its course, many of the Directory's peasant-Cossack supporters were already going over to the Bolsheviks. . . . For a few months in early 1919 there was an illusion that the two forces had joined for a common cause.[53]

Like the German-backed nationalists, the Bolsheviks squandered their potential peasant support. Where and when they were in charge, they effectively disenfranchised the middle and wealthier peasantry and instituted a new round of requisitioning. Formerly sympathetic villagers turned against the Soviets, and the final Bolshevik victory depended on support from the workers, Russian and Russified, of the cities, as well as the Donbass and the Red Army. Here the Bolsheviks were stronger than any of their contenders.

ESTONIANS The only states to remain independent after the civil war were in the northwest of Russia, along the Baltic—Poland, Finland, Estonia, Latvia, and Lithuania. Here as well, complex ethnic-class relationships existed. In the Baltic littoral, German nobles dominated rural life in areas of predominantly Estonian and Latvian peasantry. Polish and Jewish city-dwellers almost exclusively ran Vilnius, which was surrounded by Belorussian and Lithuanian villages.[54] The demographic situation in Tallinn (Reval) and Riga was even more complex. The German bourgeoisie and nobles dominated local governing institutions, but the number of Estonians and Latvians in the towns grew rapidly until the local peoples became the largest nationalities in their respective capitals.[55] Latvian and Estonian working classes and a small bourgeoisie had developed by the early twentieth century. Though they shared the burdens of an alien ruling elite, as well as the difficulty of achieving political influence under tsarism, the political trajectories of the Latvians and Estonians diverged sharply as Estonians moved toward nationalism in 1917 and Latvians turned decisively toward Bolshevism.

Estonian nationalism had developed relatively late. Influenced by the West and Central European Enlightenment, German pastors and writers first explored the culture of the Estonian *volk*. Toivo Raun and Andrejs Plakans tell us,

> The first intellectuals of Estonian origin who identified themselves as natives appeared in the 1820s, and output of publications in Estonian came to be dominated by native Estonian authors in the 1840s. For both Baltic German and Estonian intellectuals in [Hroch's] Phase A, however, it was characteristic that they had serious doubts about the Estonian capacity to develop into a modern nation.[56]

Only in the 1860s did the first generation of Estonian patriots free itself from its original German patrons. Village schoolteachers and university-educated intellectuals joined with peasants in setting up schools, forming choruses and patriotic clubs, and reading the national press. The terms *eesti rahvas* (Estonian people) and *eesti keel* (Estonian language) were adopted, first by a leading journalist, to replace the more common *maarahvas* (people of the country) and *maakeel* (language of the country).[57] Indeed, up to the turn of the century, "leading Estonian intellectuals thought of their ethnic group as a *Kulturnation* that lacked the size and capacity to become a *Staatsnation*."[58] Until 1917, the maximal goal of the national movement was autonomy within Russia, rather than independence.

The patriotic intelligentsia faced serious difficulties as it tried to penetrate the largely peasant population. Estonians had no political past with which to identify, no written language, and no national literature (though high levels of literacy predated the "national awakening"). They were kept out of educational, religious, and political institutions by the ruling Germans. Tallinn was a German town surrounded by relatively passive peasants. Yet these "disintegrating factors," as Hroch calls them, were in his view offset by "the class antagonism between the feudal German landowners and their Estonian subjects," which was "the fundamental and probably most decisive factor which from a certain date onwards stimulated the spread of national consciousness among broad strata of the oppressed Estonian nationality." Raun and Plakans, on the other hand, are wary of Hroch's use of class analysis and argue that closer study of the Estonian intelligentsia and peasantry is required before conclusions can be reached about Phase C of the Estonian national movement. The sociology of the national movement is particularly interesting. "Proprietors and tenants of average wealth were probably the main activists among the peasantry," and "rural elementary schoolteachers (there were not urban schools with Estonian as the language of instruction throughout the tsarist era) [took] the lead in promoting the national movement."[59] Moreover, religious, regional, and political factors must be integrated into an explanation. In the 1840s, tsarist officials pressured Estonian peasants to convert from Lutheranism to Orthodoxy, whereas earlier the Moravian Brethren introduced Pietism, which the Lutheran Church also saw as a threat to its faith. Not coincidentally, the Orthodox conversions and the national movement were concentrated in northern Livland.

National consciousness was further promoted in the last decades of the nineteenth century, when Estonians entered the towns, gained more education, and, along with the Latvians, achieved the highest level of literacy in the Russian empire. "The sphere of integrating factors," Hroch argues, "expanded to include the antagonism between the small-scale Estonian commodity-producers and the middle and upper German strata there."[60] The tsarist campaign of Russification in the Baltic in the last decades of the nineteenth century helped to stimulate national awareness among the broad populations of Estonians, Latvians, and Finns.

Though far less radical than the Latvians, the Estonians nevertheless gravitated toward the Bolsheviks through much of 1917. Elections to the *Maapaev* (the provincial assembly of Estonia) (May–November 1917) produced the following party alignment:[61]

Agrarian League	13	Bolsheviks	5
Labor Party	11	Radical Democrats	4
Estonian SDs		German and Swedish	
(Mensheviks)	9	minorities	2
Estonian SRs	8	Nonparty	3
Democrats (Estonian)	7		

By late July or early August, the Bolsheviks, whose greatest strength was in the larger industrial towns of Tallinn and Narva, polled 31 percent of the vote in municipal council elections (SRs, 22 percent; Estonian SD–Russian and Latvian Menshevik Bloc, 12 percent).[62] Here, as in the elections to the Tallinn soviet, a large number of voters were soldiers (16 percent in Tallinn) and non-Estonians. Bolsheviks did less well in Tartu and the rural areas. Still, in the November elections to the Constituent Assembly, the Bolsheviks outpolled the other parties (Bolsheviks, 40.2 percent; Labor Party, 21 percent), though socialists as a whole won just over 50 percent and the nonsocialists nearly matched them. Bolsheviks won in Tallinn (47.6 percent), followed by the Labor Party, but the nonsocialist Democratic Bloc won in Tartu (53.4 percent) and southern Estonia.[63]

After the October Revolution, Bolshevized soviets ran many of the towns in Estonia, but support for the soviets began to erode rapidly. The Bolsheviks were unenthusiastic about Estonian independence, failed to expropriate the estates of the Baltic barons, and tried to suppress oppositional parties. When elections were held for the Estonian Constituent Assembly in late January 1918, Bolsheviks polled only 37.1 percent of the voters, whereas the Labor Party's share rose to 29.8 percent and the Democratic Bloc held steady with 23.2 percent. The elections were incomplete, for the Bolsheviks first postponed and later cancelled them, and it appears that sentiment in the area was moving in favor of independence. When the Germans advanced in late February 1918, the nationalists used the opportunity to declare Estonia independent of Russia.

A small, compact ethnic community clearly demarcated from their German and Russian overlords and Latvian neighbors, the Estonians were nevertheless divided politically. The election data suggest that as the political situation shifted in 1917–18, Estonians adjusted their political loyalties. Socialist sentiments were strong, and anti-Russian feeling was far less apparent than anti-German. Yet the particular contingencies of the war and Bolshevik ineptitude eroded support for an all-Russian solution and helped the nationalists achieve their new goal of national independence. The small nationalist elite was able to mobilize Estonians when the Bolsheviks overplayed their hand after October, and the Germans provided the nationalists with an irresistible opportunity by backing them with force.

Group III: Latvians and Georgians

LATVIANS   Speaking a language that belongs to the Baltic branch of Indo-European languages (along with Lithuanian and Old Prussian), the ancestors of the Latvians inhabited the Baltic littoral in the ninth century. German merchants and missionaries arrived in the mid-twelfth century, and soon after, the "treacherous Livs" were converted to Christianity. The establishment of German rule obliterated the tribal structure of the indigenous peoples, and Latvians existed as a subject peasant population until the tsarist period. As with the Estonians, the German clergy dominated learning in the region and initiated scholarly interest in Latvian folk culture. A German cleric translated the Bible into Latvian in the late seventeenth century, and secular literature, written by Germans, appeared in the eighteenth. A "national awakening," that is, the development of significant secular writing by Latvians, dates from the mid-nineteenth century. Much of the ethnic "revival" actually occurred outside Latvia proper, as the title of the first Latvian newspaper, *Peterburgas avizes* (St. Petersburg Newspaper), indicates.

By the last decade of the nineteenth century, young Latvians were joining the Russian revolutionary movement— first the populists, then, after 1893, the fledgling Marxist circles. With high levels of literacy and urbanization (in 1897, 79.4 percent of the people of what would become Latvia lived in cities), as well as growing labor discontent, the Social Democrats found a ready response among both radical intellectuals and workers. Latvian parishioners resented the protectorate of the German barons over local churches and allowed the churches to be used as fora for political agitation. In Kurzeme, for example, local Social Democrats distributed socialist appeals in rural churches and developed strong ties with agricultural workers.[64]

By 1905, the Latvian Social Democratic Labor Party (LSDLP) boasted 10,000 members. Over 1,000 schoolteachers, deeply influenced by Social Democracy, met late that year and demanded instruction in the mother tongue, a more democratic curriculum, and the separation of church and education. The national struggle against the German lords combined with a broad political struggle against autocracy, led by Marxists. In the words of one veteran of the movement, "The strength of the movement was not the result of political and social factors alone . . . ; the 1905 Revolution in Latvia was also a *nationalist* revolution—a Latvian revolution against Russian-German oppression."[65]

Whereas Estonians, like Ukrainians, vacillated between nationalism and other social movements, Latvians, like Georgians, combined their ethnic and social grievances in a single, dominant socialist national movement. As Andrew Ezergailis has shown in two monographs, Social Democracy, particularly Bolshevism, had exceptionally strong support in 1917 among Latvian and other workers and among the famous Latvian riflemen. In the August elections to the municipal council of Riga, Bolsheviks won 41 percent of the vote (60 percent among ethnic Latvians).[66] A week later, Bolsheviks won 63.4 percent of the vote to the major rural institution, the Vidzeme Land Council, and in November they carried the elections to the Constituent Assembly in those parts of Latvia (Vidzeme) not yet occupied by the Germans, winning 71.85 percent of the vote. Among the *strelki* (riflemen), Bolsheviks won 95 percent of the vote.[67]

This extraordinary showing stems from a number of factors: the general Latvian alienation from the Germans and the relatively less hostile attitude toward Russians; the high proportion of landless peasants (more than 1,000,000 in 1897) that favored Social Democracy and opposed the "grey barons" (Latvian smallholders) almost as much as they did the German nobles; the support of Social Democracy by a militant working class that had experienced a bloody baptism in 1905, as well as by intellectuals, schoolteachers, and students; the particularly devastating experience of the World War, which had brought the fighting deep into Latvia, dividing the country, causing great hardship, and radicalizing the population; and finally, the ability of the Bolsheviks to develop and propagate a program that attempted to deal with both social and ethnic grievances.[68] Many Latvians in 1917 saw the solution to their national future within a Russian federation, but one that had moved beyond the bourgeois revolution. The brief experiment in Bolshevik rule after October, the Iskolat, collapsed when the Germans moved into unoccupied Latvia in February 1918. In all likelihood, Bolshevism would have been the eventual victor in Latvia save for the German intervention, which gave the nationalists a chance to create their own republic.

GEORGIANS Whereas Belorussia, Estonia, and Latvia had never been historically independent states, and Ukraine had existed more as an idea of a nation than as a unified ethnopolitical unit, Georgia, like its neighbor Armenia, had existed as a state (actually as a number of states) long before the first Russian state had been formed. The sense of a continuous existence was fundamental to the national self-conceptions of the Armenian and Georgian intelligentsias of the late eighteenth and early nineteenth centuries as they revived the study of national history and literature.

For two millennia, if not longer, Armenians and Georgians have had recognizable identities, first mentioned in the inscriptions and manuscripts of their Iranian and Greek neighbors, later (from the fifth century A.D.) in texts in their own languages. Since the fourth century A.D. they have been Christian peoples, distinct from one another once the Georgians adopted Chalcedonian orthodoxy in the sixth century, distinct from the Muslim peoples who first appeared in the seventh century and who, half a millennium later, settled in great numbers in the southern and eastern parts of Transcaucasia.[69] Though linguistically and religiously distinct, their cultures were similar, each deriving from the others, and that very closeness gave rise to disputes that continue to be present about whether the original Georgian alphabet had an Armenian origin, or whether a particular church should be attributed to a Georgian or an Armenian architect. As important as such claims to priority or originality might be to modern nationalists, the disagreements are themselves testimony both to the interpenetration of the two Christian cultures of Caucasia and to the need on the part of "patriots" to establish borders, however artificially, between them. Whatever the pedigrees attached by nationalists to ethno-religious communities of ancient times or the Middle Ages, they were quite different in self-conception and structure from modern nations. As Maxime Rodinson has pointed out,

> Before the modern epoch . . . societies of the national type—those that prefigured modern nations, extending beyond the earlier tribal structure, whatever they may be called—were characterized by extreme internal partitioning, which seems to me related quite simply to the insufficient force of the unifying factors. . . . The state still commanded limited means of action. Sub-administration, as it would be called today, was the rule and not the exception. This impelled leaders to administrate through the intermediary of multifarious bodies, sorts of sub-states that were also quasi-states.[70]

Though premodern ethnies shared a collective name, a myth of descent, a history, and a distinctive culture, though they associated themselves with a specific territory and felt a sense of solidarity, they were not as politicized, mobilized, and "territorialized" (identified with clear-cut territorial units) as nations in the modern sense are.[71] For medieval Georgians or Armenians, the primary identity was with religion and the church, the primary loyalty to the local dynast. Whether Armenian nobles lived in the Armenian heartland or in territory ruled by Georgian princes, they identified themselves and were identified by others as Armenian because they belonged to the Armenian, rather than the orthodox, church. Armenian authors referred to the land of the Armenians (*Haiastan, Haiots ashkharh, Erkir Haiots*), but they were usually speaking either about a number of polities or about a single polity that controlled only a small part of the Armenian lands.[72] In any case, the principal concern of the ecclesiastical authors of the classic histories was neither geopolitics nor territorial claims, but salvation in an otherworldly sense.[73]

Overlapping this primary loyalty was the tie to the local dynast, the *nakharar* or *azat* (Armenian), or the *mtavari* or *aznauri* (Georgian). Medieval Caucasian politics were local, infused with dynasticism and religious conflicts, and lacking a generalized, secular, ultimately territorial or ethnocultural sense of homeland or nation. Armenians might fight for Persian kings or Byzantine emperors, or even, as in A.D. 428, ask their Iranian overlord to abolish the Armenian monarchy. On the Armenian plateau, Christian princes joined Muslims or Mazdeists against their fellow Christians; and the fissiparous politics in Caucasia allowed for the larger empires to the east and the west alternately to dominate Georgia and Armenia.

The history of the Caucasian Christians diverged radically after the eleventh century, when the invasions of the Seljuk Turks pushed back the power of Byzantium and subdued the Armenians, but left the Georgians precariously independent. In the next several centuries, the Armenian nobility was cut down, some surviving for a while in the Kingdom of Lesser Armenia in Cilicia on the Mediterranean, others serving the Georgian kings as warriors, governors, or merchants. Armenia lost its political identity by the late fourteenth century, and no Armenian state would exist until 1918. In Georgia, on the other hand, the fourteenth century saw eastern Georgia (*kartli*) united with western Georgia (*imereti*) for the first time in a common state under a single monarch.[74] The modern word for Georgia (*sakartvelo*) appeared at this time. At its medieval zenith, Georgia was a multiethnic empire that included Armenians and a variety of Muslim peoples. Autonomous Georgian principalities remained under Ottoman suzerainty in the west and Iranian in the east. Only with the coming of the Russians at the beginning of the nineteenth century did the last Georgian monarchs lose their thrones.

The different experiences of the two peoples resulted in a unique ethnoclass structure in Transcaucasia. Georgians, who lived compactly in their historic territory, were largely a peasant people with a dominant noble elite that within a generation after the Russian conquest was successfully integrated into the tsarist civil and military service. Armenians, now scattered and divided between three empires (Russian, Ottoman, and Persian) were almost nowhere a compact majority—except in Erevan province, where migrations after the series of Russo-Turkish wars gave Armenians a predominant position. Without their ancient nobility, largely eliminated by the time of the Mongol occupation and the fall of the last Armenian kingdom in the late fourteenth century, Armenian merchants and manufacturers took on a highly visible role in the development of industry and trade in both Turkey and Caucasia. Baku oil was pioneered by Armenians, and the economic growth of the ancient Georgian capital, Tiflis (Tbilisi), was largely an Armenian enterprise. As the leading class among Armenians, the merchants and petty industrialists of Tiflis, Baku, Istanbul, and Izmir (Smyrna) presented non-Armenians with the most prevalent image of the Armenian. The merchant, sly and avaricious, became the stereotype of a whole people, as well as a convenient scapegoat.[75]

As they revived the study of national history and literature, the Armenian and Georgian protointelligentsias of the late eighteenth and early nineteenth centuries emphasized past glories and lost statehood. The early clerics and scholars who recovered national historiographies and compiled the first modern dictionaries and grammars were displaced in mid-century by the "sons" or "modernizers" who called for use of the vernacular language, more secularized education, and an appreciation of the "people."[76] The national emancipation began as liberal and democratic movements of writers, journalists, and teachers, but by the last decade of the nineteenth century, the second group of nationalist intellectuals had been shunted aside by younger, more radical socialists.[77] For these peoples, as for other small nations in Eastern Europe, the struggle for national emancipation was also a struggle against the non-national or denationalized bourgeoisie, against the effects of an imperializing capitalism, and for full participation in a modern, European life.

Though the similarities between the origins and initial stages of Armenian and Georgian nationalism are striking, the different social structures and political imperatives of the two nationalities led to quite different nationalist ideologies and political evolutions. Georgians, like the Latvians, developed a socialist nationalist intelligentsia that successfully based a mass political movement on the ethnic working class and the local peasantry. Armenians, on the other hand, were profoundly affected by their division between three great empires, and by the immediate threat to national survival presented by their Muslim neighbors.

Largely a rural people, Georgians were divided between a peasant majority and a declining nobility that had survived the annexation of Georgia by the Russians and in time became part of the *dvorianstvo* (Russian gentry). But the noble elite failed to make a successful adjustment to the post-Emancipation economy, and their ideal of national harmony cutting across classes failed to attract followers beyond the intelligentsia.

With the nobility losing its dominant economic and political position and the towns dominated by Armenian merchants and artisans who had formed the Caucasian middle class since the Middle Ages, the Georgian intelligentsia, themselves the offspring of a declassé nobility, turned to a radical analysis of Georgia's condition. In the 1890s, Georgian intellectuals adopted a specifically Marxist worldview that saw both the bourgeoisie (which in this case was largely Armenian) and the autocracy (which was Russian) as enemies of Georgian social and political freedom. Given the particular composition of Georgia's society, the social and national struggles were successfully merged under a Marxist leadership that claimed not to be nationalist and was willing to link up with all-Russian Social Democracy.

The natural constituency for Georgian Social Democrats, the workers, was supplemented by 1905 by broad support (almost unique in the Russian empire) among the peasantry. By the years of the first revolution, Georgian Marxist intellectuals found themselves at the head of a genuinely supraclass national liberation movement. The Mensheviks easily won the elections to the four state *dumas*, controlled soviets and councils in the towns and countryside in 1917, and were the overwhelming choice of Georgians in the elections to the Constituent Assembly. In Georgia the development of a mass national movement (Hroch's Phase C) had been achieved in the first decade of the twentieth century, but instead of a vertically integrating nationalism, Georgians adopted an expressly non-nationalist socialist movement.

With the October Revolution, the Georgian Mensheviks acted swiftly to disarm the Russian garrison in Tiflis and establish local soviet power. Refusing to recognize the Bolshevik government in Petrograd, the Transcaucasian socialist parties (with the exception of the local Bolsheviks) gradually separated the region from the rest of Russia by first declaring autonomy, later independence for the whole of Transcaucasia, and finally the establishment of three separate independent republics. Certainly the most viable and stable state in Transcaucasia was Georgia. Here Social Democracy was well grounded in both the working class and the peasantry. German intervention was needed to prevent attack from outside, not to shore up the regime.

Ironically, the Georgian nation-state was formed and led by Marxists who had expected a democratic revolution in Russia that would solve at one sweep the people's ethnic and social oppression. Instead, the Marxists found themselves at the head of an independent "bourgeois" state, the managers of the "democratic revolution" in one small country, called upon to fulfill the national programs of parties far to their right. Unquestionably they had excellent chances for success—the Mensheviks had the support of the great majority of the Georgian people—but the larger imperatives of the central Soviet government did not permit them to demonstrate the potential for democratic socialism in a postrevolutionary state. By 1920, a powerful group within the Bolshevik party pushed for an uprising within Georgia, to be followed by an invasion by the Red Army. Lenin was initially opposed to this cynical disregard for the evident influence of the Georgian Social Democrats, but he backed down in face of the fait accompli engineered by Orjonikidze and Stalin.

The parallels between Latvian and Georgian experiences are striking. In both countries, the older generation of national patriots (in Latvia, "Young Latvia"; in Georgia, the *pirveli dasi* [first group] and the *meore dasi* [second group]) were supplanted by Marxists (the Latvian "New Current" and the Georgian *mesame dasi* [third group]). National hostility was directed toward the locally dominant nationality (in Latvia, the Germans; in Georgia, the Armenians), rather than toward the Russians. Independence resulted from political circumstances, rather than from the plans or intentions of the dominant political movement. In both countries, class and ethnic identities overlapped and reinforced one another, but the form of expression was socialist rather than predominantly nationalist.

Group IV: Finns

Finland is a unique case of a widespread commitment to the nationalist program, first of autonomy, then of independence, with the leading role in 1917 played by the Social

Democratic party. Political unity around the question of independence, however, was marred by deep social divisions
between those groups which supported the socialists and
those which voted for the nonsocialist parties. Risto Alapuro writes,

> Although ultimate control was exercised in St. Petersburg [in the
> tsarist period], domination within the country—political, eco-
> nomic, and cultural—was in the hands not of the Russians but
> of the Swedish-speaking upper class. Thus, although linguistic,
> social, and educational barriers coincided within Finland, the lo-
> cal elite was not an extension of the metropolitan elite.[78]

The position of the Swedish speakers—nobles, bureaucrats,
and middle-class elements—was similar to that of the German nobles in the Baltic and of the Polish landlords in Lithuania, but the Swedish speakers had never enjoyed feudal
privileges, did not have control over land, and exercised their
hegemony through the bureaucracy and the literary culture.

Though the status of Finns as a subordinate people within
a region in which they composed the majority echoes the
social position of most non-Russian peoples in the nineteenth century, the unique juridical status of Finland provided a radically different political environment for the development of Finnish nationality. From its incorporation
into the Russian empire in 1809, Finland, which had never
been an historic state, achieved the status of an autonomous
polity, with its own local Diet, a Senate at the apex of the
bureaucracy, guarantees for the Lutheran religion, and the
continuance of the Fundamental Laws of the Swedish period. Emperor Alexander I declared himself Grand Duke of
Finland and was formally recognized by the Diet. He pledged
to observe the constitution and laws of Finland. For the
next eighty-odd years, Finland existed as a constitutional
anomaly within the empire, a distinct country with its own
army, legal system, currency, and taxation, separated from
the rest of the empire by tariffs and a frontier.[79]

Thanks to tsarist policy, the Finns were for the first time in their history "tied to each other through a domestic administration."[80] Autonomy within the empire "stimulated a feeling of mutual interdependence among the inhabitants of Finland."[81] Thus, the peoples of Finland experienced a process not unlike that of Western European nation-building, where states formed around an ethnic core that had already consolidated before the formation of a national consciousness.

Though distinctions remained between the privileged "Swedes" and the "Finns," the geographic and political unity of the country, the economic ties between Finnish towns and the countryside, the creation of a "national market" in Finland, and the relative weakness of social and class conflicts in the nineteenth century created a sense of Finnish nationality that included both Swedish and Finnish speakers. "Finland was one of the few relatively 'overdeveloped' minority regions within the multinational empires of the time," like Bohemia, Croatia, and Russian Poland.[82] Relative prosperity for larger farmers and the forest industry undermined the position of the gentry, as in Georgia, and gave rise to a Finnish industrial working class "rooted firmly in the countryside."[83]

Still a largely agricultural country until the middle of the twentieth century, Finland's industrial work force made up about 10 percent of the population around 1900. By World War I, only 15 percent of the 3,000,000 Finns lived in towns or cities. These percentages were higher than in Russia proper, but lower than in much of Scandinavia and Western Europe.[84] As in the history of other European working classes, an urban Finnish work force existed before the establishment of free wage labor under capitalism. Artisans and the first factory workers understood that they were different from the upper and middle classes and had distinct social duties to perform, though they had no sense of class solidarity. Social differences, writes Pertti Haapala, were considered personal matters, unaffected by the social system. Until the early twentieth century, Finnish workers, many of them emigrants from the landless peasantry, were so heterogeneous that "the fact of being a worker was not as such sufficient to create a *common* notion of working class identity."[85]

The formation of a Finnish working class was intimately connected to aspirations by the lower class and the intelligentsia

> to assert their own social identity against that of the (Swedish-speaking) upper class. The Finnish labour movement was born in this context. Indeed, one cannot understand the nature and the development of that movement unless one sees it as a part of the organization of the *nation* as such. At the beginning of the twentieth century the social question, the language question and the Russian question were all intertwined with each other to such an extent that in the thinking of the working-class Finnish national consciousness, democracy, autonomy and socialism differed hardly at all from each other.[86]

The first generation to advocate Finnish culture and language came from the Swedish-speaking elite. In 1835, Finnish folk poems were compiled into the *Kalevala*, which was celebrated as the Finnish national epic and provided an heroic ingredient for a new Finnish identity.[87] In the 1840s and 1850s, Swedish speakers, like the philosopher J. V. Snellman, advocated use of the Finnish language by all classes in Finland, and in the 1860s and 1870s, educated workers cooperated with the patriots to set up schools and cultural organizations to spread the new nationalism. By the end of the century, the upward mobility of Finnish speakers and the linguistic adaptation of the elites encouraged the peoples of Finland to share a single national conception. Finland was understood to be a unique political and geographic entity with its own national culture. Socially, however, the country remained divided between the Swedish-speaking bureaucracy and bourgeoisie on one side and the bulk of the population, Finnish-speaking, on the other. Finnish workers

gradually grew away from their former bourgeois and intellectual allies, and in the new century the majority of the
workers identified with the Social Democratic intellectuals.

As political nationalisms were increasingly perceived by
tsarist officials as threats to the unity of the empire, the Russian autocracy began to see the autonomy of the Grand
Duchy of Finland as an intolerable anomaly. In 1890, the
Finnish postal system was incorporated into the all-Russian
system. In 1899, Finland's separate military units were integrated into the empire's, and that same year the young emperor, Nicholas II, provoked the Finns by declaring that
henceforth Finnish legislation that concerned the empire as
a whole was to be reviewed by his Council of Ministers before being sanctioned by the tsar. Russian was to be an official language in Finland, and Russians—whom the Finns
considered *perivihollinen* (hereditary enemies)—were to be
granted full citizenship rights in the Grand Duchy. In this
way the Diet was to be reduced to a mere advisory body. The
next year, the use of Russian was extended to the Finnish
administration at the expense of Swedish.

Half a million Finns signed a protest, and much hostility
formerly targeted at Swedes was now aimed at the Russians.
The Young Finns and the Swedish party resisted the Russian
inroads, and after the general strike that swept Russia and
Finland in October 1905, Nicholas was forced to restore Finland's former rights.[88] Most importantly for its future political development, Finland became the first country in Europe
to be granted universal suffrage, the first in which women
voted alongside men.

In the elections to the Diet in 1907, the Social Democrats
won 34 percent of the urban vote and 38 percent of the rural
vote, achieving the largest representation of any socialist
party in Europe. In 1916, the Finnish Social Democrats became the first socialist party in the world to win an absolute
majority in the legislature. "In the Social Democratic oppo-

sition to Russian autocracy, national and class aspects were necessarily linked."[89] But unlike the victorious Left in Georgia (or in Latvia in 1917), the Finnish Social Democrats were neither able nor particularly anxious to overwhelm their conservative opponents.

In the first year of revolution, the Finnish socialists became the principal advocates of Finland's independence from Russia. In one of its first acts, the Provisional Government restored the constitution of the Grand Duchy of Finland. The manifesto emphasized the illegality of tsarist regulations that contradicted the laws of Finland and recognized the full "internal independence" of the former Grand Duchy. At the same time, however, it declared the Petrograd government "the possessor of full sovereign power." The Social Democratic leadership of the Finnish parliament soon proposed that with the fall of the monarchy, sovereignty should pass to the Finnish government, while conceding that the Provisional Government would continue to decide foreign and military policy for the time being. The future Bolshevik Otto Kuusinen concluded that this draft constitution gave Finland "all that one could wish and is better than independence."[90] The reaction in Petrograd to the Finnish move, however, was quick, sharp, and negative. Russian policy, as initially formulated by Kerensky, rejected any firm pronouncement on the ultimate status of Finland until the convening of the All-Russian Constituent Assembly. When in early April the Finnish Social Democrats met with the Russian Menshevik leaders, the latter recognized Finland's right to self-determination, but also held that only the Constituent Assembly could ultimately determine the issue. The only major party to support Finland's full independence was the Bolsheviks.

As early as March 11, Lenin, still in Switzerland, had argued that "the Russian proletariat will guarantee to a Finnish republic complete freedom, including the freedom to secede." His principled support of the right of national self-determination, including secession, involved a peculiar confidence that granting such freedom would lead to trust among the non-Russians and their willingness to remain within the new Russian state. Lenin told the Seventh Conference of the Bolsheviks in April: "Our attitude toward the separatist movement is indifferent, neutral. . . . We are for Finland receiving complete freedom because then there will be greater trust in Russian democracy, and the Finns will not separate."

The attitude of the Petrograd authorities stimulated even more support for independence in Finland, and through May and June the Finnish Social Democrats pushed for a law (the *valtalaki*) that ascribed sovereignty to the Finnish Diet. Their understanding was that the law conformed to the position taken by the First All-Russian Congress of Soviets (the report of the Abramovich Commission), but in fact the Russian socialists were hoping to delay the final disposition of Finland until the Constituent Assembly, and the Finnish socialists were impatient to achieve a declaration of independence as soon as possible.

Until the very last days of its existence, the Provisional Government refused to concede full independence to Finland and proved willing to use armed force to enforce its policy in Finland. The delays in establishing an authoritative government in Helsinki aided the process of deepening social division in Finland that would eventually lead to a bloody civil war. The English historian of Finland's revolution, Anthony F. Upton, concludes bitterly:

> The refusal of Kerenski, partly for reasons of personal pride, to consider any proposal that involved formal recognition of the valtalaki [Finnish declaration of independence], though he was ready to concede the substance of the law, deprived Finland of this last chance to draw back from open class struggle: It was one more in the catalogue of palpable blunders for which Kerenski has to answer.[91]

By autumn, the country was dividing between moderate "bourgeois" parties that called for law and order and were hesitant about the break with Russia, the Social Democratic majority that campaigned for independence, and Bolshevized Russian soldiers. Red Guards made up of workers sympathetic to the socialists clashed with Home Guards, many of whom were pro-German and virulently antisocialist. A general strike called by the Social Democrats followed the Bolshevik takeover in Petrograd, and revolutionary councils were set up. As the Finnish Social Democrats wavered before Bolshevik urgings to seize power, conservative forces were able to mobilize the rural population against the urban workers. Left without peasant support, the workers now found themselves politically isolated from almost all other social groups.

On December 6, 1917, Finland became an independent state, recognized by the new Soviet government in Petrograd. The newly formed Finnish army, under General Mannerheim, began to disarm Russian troops. Fearing the loss of the revolutionary gains of 1917, workers and socialists prepared to defend Helsinki. Aligned with the German army, the Finnish Whites launched a brutal attack on the socialists and the Red Guard to eliminate their hold on the capital and on southern Finland. The Germans took the capital in April, and by early May the whole of Finland was in White or German hands. In the fighting, 3,500 Reds were killed, 78 percent of them workers. In the subsequent White Terror, 200 people a day were killed, and 12,500 Red prisoners died in prison camps.[92] The upper and middle classes, most of the intellectuals, and the independent peasantry backed the Whites, whereas workers and landless peasants joined the Reds. Middle and poor peasants and crofters remained largely passive.

In Finland, then, we find yet another variant of the class/nationality relationship: by late 1917, all social groups favored independence, but the common national program could not overcome class and regional cleavages. The result was a bloody civil war; the defeat of the Social Democrats, who had led the struggle for democracy and independence; and the coming to power of a conservative, pro-German elite. Finland's political and cultural development in the nineteenth and early twentieth centuries had created both a Finnish nation and a coherent and conscious working class. For the first decade and a half of this century, their political agendas coincided, but in 1917, a bitter struggle for dominance in Finland shattered their close collaboration. Once the Russian enemy was removed, internal social tensions turned Finn against Finn. "Independence," concludes Anthony F. Upton,

> had been proclaimed, fought for, and then willfully cast aside, for Red Finland would have been a satellite of Soviet Russia, and White Finland had become a dependency of imperial Germany. Certainly most White Finns, and many others, regarded a German overlordship as preferable to that of Russia, but still what they had got [by May 1918] was a mockery of an independent state.[93]

Group V: Armenians

The Armenian experience as a geographically divided and endangered people led at first to a peculiar form of "nonterritorial nationalism": the Armenians were an imagined community that shared a culture, a history, and a language, but had lost its hold on its historic homeland. Within the Russian empire, Armenians were scattered in urban centers, with a relatively compact peasantry in Erevan province. At the same time, an influential diaspora connected the educated and business people of Anatolia and Transcaucasia with Europe, the Middle East, and even India. Here, then, was an historic nation with an educated urban bourgeoisie, disconnected socially and by virtue of distance or international borders from the heartland of its own people, which lay in eastern Anatolia.

Despite the increase in Armenians in absolute terms in the nineteenth and early twentieth centuries and their continued economic and political dominion over the largest cities of the Caucasus, Armenians increasingly perceived themselves to be in a vulnerable demographic and political position. The relative status of the largest Armenian community, that of the Armenian plateau of eastern Anatolia, worsened with the rapid growth of the Kurdish population, the in-migration of Balkan Muslims, Circassians, and other Muslims from the Caucasus, and the out-migration of Armenians, particularly after the massacres of 1894–96. Already in the minority within a heavily Turkish and Kurdish population, now even more the victims of Muslim competitors for land and influence, Armenians in Turkey in the 1870s and 1880s filed numerous complaints and petitions with Ottoman officials and Western diplomatic representatives. But the turn toward Europe only antagonized Turkish officials and led to the growing sense that Armenians were a foreign, subversive element in the sultan's realm.

Impressed by the urgency of a political solution, the Armenian intelligentsia of the Russian empire directed its efforts toward their conationals in Turkey. In contrast to the Georgians, the Armenian revolutionary parties, founded at the end of the 1880s and the beginning of the 1890s, disavowed joint solutions with other parties of the Russian empire and sent their cadres to organize in Turkey. By means of "propaganda of the deed" and examples of militant sacrifice, Armenian revolutionaries attempted to mobilize a rather passive and demoralized peasantry in western Armenia, while at the same time inciting Western powers to come to the aid of beleaguered Christians. Though there were a number of spectacular examples of "resistance" by armed Armenians (Zeitun, Sassun), the revolutionaries never achieved mass mobilization. At the turn of the century, they cooperated with Turkish oppositionists, precursors of the Young Turks, in the hope that an Armenian future within the Ottoman empire would be secured with the overthrow of Abdul Hamid II and the establishment of a constitutional regime.

The self-destruction of one major Armenian party (the Social Democratic *Hnchak* [Bell] party) and the relative isolation of the liberals and "internationalist" Social Democrats in the cities left the more nationalist of the socialist parties, the Armenian Revolutionary Federation (*Hai Heghapoghakan Dashnaktsutiun*), as the only real contender for Armenian loyalties by the early twentieth century. In 1903 it also gained wide support among city dwellers, and even among peasants in the Caucasus, as the principal defender of the Church, whose properties had been requisitioned by the tsarist government in that year.

The outbreak of World War I and the genocide of Armenians in eastern Anatolia created an entirely new situation, however. In the spring of 1915, missionaries and diplomats, travelers and victims, reported that the Turkish military was systematically murdering adult male Armenians and forcibly deporting hundreds of thousands of others. Though the exact number of those killed or forcibly deported may never be known, estimates run from 600,000 to 2,500,000 Armenian deaths in the years 1915–22. Whatever the exact dimensions of the genocide, Armenians suffered a demographic disaster that shifted the center of their population from the heartland of historic Armenia to the relatively safer eastern regions held by the Russians. Tens of thousands of refugees fled to the Caucasus with the retreating Russian armies, and the cities of Baku and Tiflis filled with Armenians from Turkey.

Armenian volunteer military units fought on the Caucasian front, and when Russian troops "voted with their feet" late in 1917 and abandoned the Caucasus, Armenians found that they possessed one of the most powerful military forces in the region. The principal threats to the Armenians came from their ethnic and religious enemies, the Ottoman Turks and the Azerbaijanis, and the very acuity of those threats completed what two decades of revolutionary propaganda had been working to accomplish—the effective mobilization of the Caucasian Armenian population to vote and fight for the national future as defined by the *Dashnaktsutiun*.

Tensions rose in the Caucasian cities as the new immigrants added to the wartime pressures on the limited resources of the tsar's collapsing empire. Yet ethnic conflicts were far less frequent than social clashes throughout the first year of revolution. Nevertheless, Armenians, traumatized by the mass killings and deportations in Turkey, maintained their separate national agenda, forming their own political national council in Tiflis. As economic pressures and the question of state power, along with the issue of the war, relegated ethnic matters to second place, Armenians hoped that constitutional reforms would grant them a degree of autonomy and self-rule within a democratic Russia. Though ethnic fractures appeared in the newly elected municipal *duma* in Tiflis, as Georgians replaced the formerly hegemonic Armenian middle class, they were contained within a political framework that promised democratic solutions to these perennial problems. But the Bolshevik victory in Petrograd, their relative strength in Baku and weakness in Tiflis, and the removal of Russian troops from the Caucasian front and urban garrisons created a new political environment in which the possibility of Turkish invasion threatened some nationalities (the Armenians) and was seen as an opportunity by others (the Azerbaijanis). Armenians voted overwhelmingly for the Dashnaks in the elections to the Constituent Assembly.

The nationalities had to choose between Soviet Russia, the Entente, or the Germans, and each national leadership chose a different path. The central political issue became self-defense, and in the context of Russian retreat and Turkish-German advance it quickly took on an ethnic dimension. A brief experiment in Transcaucasian autonomy was followed by an even briefer one in an independent federative republic. By late May 1918, the Georgians had opted for the Germans rather than the Bolsheviks; the Azerbaijanis had turned expectantly toward the Turks; the multinational city of Baku had chosen Soviet power; and the Armenians were left to their fate.[94]

The only realistic hope for an ethnic Armenian homeland in the postgenocide period was the small enclave around Erevan, which in May 1918 became the center of a fragile independent republic. Armenian political leaders had not been anxious to attempt independence, but now they were forced to take control of their refugee population. They alone of the Transcaucasian peoples turned to the Entente for support. The ostensibly socialist ideology of the *Dashnaktsutiun* was largely neglected, and the party became the representative of all classes of Caucasian Armenians as they faced together the common threat from Ottoman and post-Ottoman Turks. Class divisions had become irrelevant as a reluctantly independent Armenia, a tiny enclave of migrants, refugees, and local people, attempted to provide a last refuge for Armenians.

Conclusion

The revolution of 1917 and the subsequent civil war were interpreted by the Marxists as a civil war of class against class, worker against peasant and bourgeois, city against country. Many Bolsheviks and other Russian socialist and nonsocialist parties viewed events as a single, gigantic revolutionary process engulfing the whole of the now-defunct empire. Nationalists, in contrast, interpreted the struggle as a national war of Russians against minorities, the center against the peripheries. They viewed the experiences of the borderlands as unique events that fulfilled and justified the natural historical evolution to national independence.

The nationalists' example, followed by most of the monographic studies of individual nationalities in the West, has produced histories of the non-Russian peripheries sharply distinguished from those of central Russia. Whereas much of the new social history depicts the revolution in the central Russian cities as a struggle between increasingly polarized social classes, or at least an intense pulling-apart of the *verkhi* (top) and the *nizy* (bottom) of society, historians of the revolution in the borderlands have traditionally emphasized ethnic rather than social struggles.[95] Yet woven through the monographic literature on the non-Russian regions, both Soviet and Western, is a red thread of social conflict of great intensity in the national borderlands, obscured at times by the ethnic coloration, but in fact made all the more ferocious by cultural as well as class cleavages. Here the social and the ethnic are so closely intertwined that separation of the two can be artificial and misleading.

When we acknowledge the provisional and contingent nature of nationality and class and the volatility with which people moved from social to ethnic identities and loyalties, the revolution and civil war, both in the center and in the peripheries, appear much more related than divorced. It was not two kinds of revolution, but one gigantic social upheaval that engulfed the whole of the Russian empire in the third year of the World War, bringing down the integrating imperial authority and launching a crisis of authority that continued well into the civil-war years. For that period, economic disintegration shredded the social fabric of the old order. Everyone everywhere was affected, and physical survival became the primary goal for tens of millions of people. Ethnically distinct peasants and workers, whatever their particular experiences, shared the general experience of the collapse of state authority and economic order. The sundering of political and economic ties opened the way for some parts of the empire, most immediately Finland and Poland, to opt for a viable independence (though not without dissenters and, in the case of Finland, bloody civil war); other areas, fatally linked to the whole history of Russia, were simply set adrift (like Azerbaijan and Armenia) or found neither the opportunity nor the will to break with revolutionary Russia (for example, Tataria).

The story of national formation and nationalism in the revolutionary years is seen here as part of the intricate mosaic of the Russian Civil War, with social and ethnic conflicts inextricably mixed. The civil war in the disintegrating Russian empire was a civil war everywhere, right up to pre–World War I borders, and though in the national peripheries the conflict took on aspects of national wars, the social struggles between workers and industrialists, *tsentsovoe obshchestvo* (propertied society) and *demokratiia* (the lower classes), city and countryside were powerfully present. From this "civil-war perspective," Soviet power or Bolshevism never simply meant Russia, and the extension of its power was not simply a Russian conquest of other peoples. Bolshevism, for better or worse, was the actual achievement of the revolution of the *demokratiia* of the central Russian cities as that revolution stood after October 1917; Russian and Russified Ukrainian workers in Kiev and Kharkov, Russians and Armenians in Baku, and Russians and Latvians in Riga supported local soviet power (and even Bolshevism) in preference to a national independence promoted by a small nationalist elite in the name of a peasant majority. The difficult choice before both the Russians and the non-Russian peoples was whether to support the central Soviet government and the revolution as now defined by it, or to accept a precarious existence in alliance with undependable allies from abroad with their own self-aggrandizing agendas. In making that choice, social structure, past experience, and the relative advantages of the options available were often much more significant than ethnic considerations.

Almost everywhere, the nationalist movements were either strengthened or fatally weakened by the nature of their class base. Because ethnic solidarity, activism, Russophilia, or Russophobia were very often primed by social discontents, where nationalist leaderships were able to combine social reform with their programs of self-definition, autonomy, or independence, their chances for success were increased. Where social, particularly agrarian, reform was delayed or neglected, ethnic political aspirations alone did not prove strong enough to sustain nationalist intellectuals in power. For ethnic leaders who faced a peasant majority indifferent to their claims to power and caught up in an uneven struggle with the Bolsheviks, an appeal to the Great Powers of Central and Western Europe became the last resort. And the intervention of foreigners, particularly the Germans in the crucial first months after the October Revolution, radically altered the developmental lines of the first revolutionary year. Geoff Eley writes,

> By interposing itself between the peoples of the Russian Empire and their practical rights of self-determination at a crucial moment of revolutionary political rupture—after the old order had collapsed, but while the new was still struggling to be born (to adapt a saying of Gramsci)—the German military administration suspended the process of democratic experimentation before it had hardly begun. The Germans' essentially destructive impact explains some of the difficulty experienced by the competing political leaderships in the western borderlands of Russia during 1918–20 in creating a lasting relationship to a large enough coalition of social support. The various political forces—Bolshevik, left-nationalist, autonomist, separatist, counter-revolutionary—operated more or less in a political vacuum in a fragile and indeterminate relationship to the local population, not just because the Belorussian and Ukrainian societies were so "backward" (the explanation normally given), but

because the cumulative effects of war, Imperial collapse, and German occupation had radically dislocated existing social organization, strengthening old antagonisms between groups and inaugurating new ones.[96]

Nationalism, like class consciousness, was a disturbingly ephemeral phenomenon among most non-Russians in these turbulent years, especially once the revolution outgrew the cities. Whatever their cultural and ethnographic preferences, non-Russian peasants did not automatically opt for the national programs of their urban ethnic leaders. Mobilized in the aftermath of the October Revolution, the peasantry was, in Eley's words, "a class restlessly *in motion.*"[97] Neither nationality nor class had an a priori claim on the loyalties of its potential constituents.

The mixed fates of nationalism and socialism in the whirlwind of the Russian Revolution and the subsequent civil war are illustrative of the relationships of class and nationality, both to the historical social locations of peoples and to the social and intellectual activities that harmonize internal discordances within groups and imagine interconnections between members of the group and the distance from the "other." Neither "objective" in the sense of existing outside the constitutive practices of its members and its opponents, nor completely "subjective" in the sense of existing only when perceived to exist by members or opponents, a nationality or a social class is here understood to be both socially and discursively constituted.

In the great sweep of the revolution and civil war, nationalism was for most nationalities still largely concentrated among the ethnic intelligentsia, the students, and the lower middle classes of the towns, with at best a fleeting following among broader strata. Among Belorussians, Lithuanians, and Azerbaijanis, the paramount identification was not with one's nation, but with people nearby with whom one shared social and religious community. Neither nationalism nor socialism was able to mobilize large numbers of these peoples into the political struggles that would decide their future. For several other nationalities, among them the Latvians and the Georgians, class-based socialist movements were far more potent than political nationalism. Socialism as presented by the dominant intellectual elite answered the grievances of both social and ethnic inferiority and promised a sociopolitical solution to the dual oppression. For still other nationalities, like the Ukrainians and the Estonians, nationality competed with class for the primary loyalty of the workers and peasants, with neither winning a dominant position. In Finland, a deadly polarization between social groups led to a civil war between parts of a population relatively united on the question of national independence and commitment to Finnish culture. For the Armenians, a rather unique case of a people divided between two empires, without a secure area of concentration, and facing imminent extermination, a nonclass, vertically integrating nationalism overwhelmed all competitors.

The reasons for the relative weakness of nationalism and the strength of local and social identities in 1917–18, and even further into the civil war, require further attention by scholars, but tentatively one might suggest that the social distance between villagers and townspeople, between peasants and intellectuals, mitigated against the supraclass appeal of nationalism. The most successful appeals were populist or even socialist, especially when they were enhanced by ethnic arguments. Furthermore, long-established trade patterns and complex economic relations tied most of the non-Russian peoples of the old empire to the center (the Finns and the Poles are perhaps exceptions here); these were powerful forces for integration with the rest of Russia rather than for the development of separate nations. Separation from Russia was almost always a political decision based on a need for support by an outside power—at first Germany and Turkey, later the Entente powers—and had far less intrinsic appeal among the various nationalities than has been customarily assumed.

The ebbs and flows of socialism and nationalism were tied to the tides of war and revolution, to the relative fates of the Great Powers and their ability to act within Russia. In the twentieth century, intervention has become an unwelcome but ubiquitous guest at the revolutionary table. When the Bolsheviks were relatively weak and the Germans strong, separatism and the fortunes of the nationalists rose; when the Germans were defeated and the Entente withdrew, the appeals of the Bolsheviks for social revolution, land to the peasants, and even a kind of greater "all-Russia nationalism" found supporters. Not to be discounted as a factor in the Bolshevik victory was their own confidence in their reading of history, their sensitivity to the social dynamics within the revolutionary crises, their readiness to compromise with popular nationalism in the formation of the Soviet federation, and their willingness to use their military and political power ruthlessly to achieve their historic goals.

Lenin's estimation that national separatism would be reduced by central Russian tolerance and a willingness to allow national self-determination to the point of independence has appeared, understandably, to be either a utopian fantasy or an example of political dissimulation. Yet Lenin appears to have understood that for many ordinary people, neither nationalism nor a sense of class was an end in itself as often was the case for intellectuals. If, in fact, nationalism was far weaker than most nationalists have allowed; if in Russia it was almost invariably connected with concrete social and political discontents caused by years of discrimination and hardship under tsarism; and if, indeed, significant groups within the non-Russian peoples responded well to the socialist programs of social transformation and national self-determination; then perhaps Lenin's notion that non-Russians would be willing to remain within a multinational state was less a fantasy than another example of his political style, an uneasy combination of hard-nosed realism and the willingness to take extraordinary risks.

CHAPTER 3

State-Building and Nation-Making: The Soviet Experience

In an illuminating chapter, "Revolution over Asia," E. H. Carr notes the assimilation of the "national question" to the "colonial" issue in the Bolshevik discourse. Colonial policy was

> a logical corollary and a natural extension of national policy; the theoretical foundations of both were the same. . . . Soviet policy appealed in one broad sweep to the peoples of Asia as a whole, to the former subjects of the Tsar, to the subjects of other empires and to the nominally independent dependencies of the capitalist world-market.[1]

Already in the appeal "To All Muslim Toilers of Russia and the East," issued just one month after the Bolsheviks came to power, the powerful rhetoric of self-determination, liberation, independence, and anti-imperialism established a unity of the struggle against colonial and national oppression. Since the Red Army was engaged for much of the period of the Russian Civil War in a simultaneous battle against "bourgeois nationalists" and "foreign interventionists," anti-imperialism was not distinguished from the drive to "liberate" the former subject peoples of the Russian empire. Soviet Russia was conceived not as an ordinary national state but as the first stone in a future multinational socialist edifice. The reach of the Russian Revolution was to be limitless. What its enemies would later build into a potent ideological image of a drive toward world domination was in its incarnation an effort directed primarily against British imperialism. It brought Lenin and his comrades into a series of peculiar alliances with the fallen Turkish leader Enver Pasha, King Amanullah of Afghanistan, the rebel Kuchuk Khan in northern Persia, Kemal Pasha in Anatolia, and other nonsocialist nationalists. The empires of the Europeans in Asia, the semicolonial periphery of Persia, China, and Turkey (in Lenin's conceptualization), and the newly independent national states established after the October Revolution, dependent as they were on the presence and support of European power, all were linked in a single understanding as the last props of a moribund capitalism. With a confidence born of recent victories and faith in a Marxist eschatology, and with an opportunism rooted in the limited resources at hand, the Bolsheviks used all the means available to realize their dream of international revolution. For Communists of the civil-war period, internationalism was less the servant of the Soviet state than the Soviet state was the servant of internationalism.

From the very beginning, the pull between nationalism and socialism was a struggle between supporters of the Soviet government and foreign interventionists who hoped to gain allies in the war against the Reds. A pristine nationalism, able to establish a firm base of support in the ethnic population and to hold on to political independence without foreign help, was difficult to find in the peripheries of the Russian empire. Two fiercely antagonistic discourses contended in a battle of rhetoric and violence: nationalists appealed to the West to defend their right to national self-determination against a renewed Russian threat, whereas Communists portrayed the nationalists and their foreign backers as part of an imperialist endeavor to contain or destroy Bolshevism and the coming international revolution.

At the beginning of the twentieth century, when Social Democrats agonized over the emerging "national question," Russian Marxists sought both to win allies among the non-Russian nationalities and to combat the nationalists' attempts to splinter the unitary state. Secure in their faith in Marx's assertions that "national differences and antagonisms between peoples are vanishing gradually from day to day" and that "the supremacy of the proletariat will cause them to vanish still faster," Bolshevik theorists were opposed to political solutions that would divert what they understood to be the flow of history and promote ethnic identity. Lenin, Stalin, Armenian Bolshevik Stepan Shahumian, and others were adamant in their opposition to federalism, to the Austromarxist principle of "extraterritorial national cultural autonomy" (each nationality represented in parliament no matter where its members live), and to the moderate nationalist principle of "territorial national cultural autonomy" (ethnicity defining autonomous territorial political units). Leninists preferred "regional autonomy," in which political units would not have ethnic designations. The "proletarian solution" to the nationality question would preserve the unitary state while allowing for local self-government and guaranteeing complete cultural and linguistic freedom within the socialist state. Although national self-determination for Lenin meant that a nationality could choose to become fully independent, in his pre-1917 formulation nationalities that stayed within the socialist state would have neither the right to an autonomous political territory nor the right to a federative relationship to the center.

The Bolsheviks' prerevolutionary thinking on the national

question did not survive the revolution intact. The new Soviet state was both federative, at least in name and theory, and based on ethnic political units. Indeed, for more than a decade following the civil war, nationalities like the Jews and Armenians, and the Ukrainians in Russia, enjoyed extraterritorial privileges, with their own schools and soviets operating in republics of other nationalities. Soviet practice was a compromise with maximal ideological desiderata. And the very expectation that such concessions to the national principle would lead to the consolidation of ethnicity, rather than to its disappearance, proved to be correct for the larger nationalities. Rather than a melting pot, the Soviet Union became the incubator of new nations.

Though many of his comrades consistently favored subordinating nationalism strictly to class considerations, Lenin was both aware of the power of nationalism (even as he hoped to harness it to the proletarian revolution) and ready to concede the need to ally with "bourgeois nationalists." For Lenin, nationalism and separatism were neither natural nor inevitable, but were contingent on the sense of oppression that nationalities experienced from imperialism. He remained convinced that nationalism reflected only the interests of the bourgeoisie, that the proletariat's true interests were supranational, and that the end of colonialism would diminish the power of nationalist sentiments.[2] In contrast to his party comrades on the Left, he refused to oppose the independence of Finland, Poland, and Ukraine. Though he hoped that such separations could be avoided and reserved the option to oppose specific moves toward independence on principle, he abjured the use of force to keep the empire whole. He was unequivocal in his public commitment to "the full right of separation from Russia of all nations and nationalities, oppressed by tsarism, joined by force or held by force within the borders of the state, i.e., annexed." At the same time, he argued that the goal of the proletarian party was the creation of the largest state possible and the rapprochement (*sblizhenie*) and eventual merging (*sliianie*) of nations. Such a goal was to be reached, not through force, but voluntarily, by the will of the workers. Already in early 1917, Lenin moderated his earlier position and proposed that full regional (and national) autonomy be guaranteed in the new state.[3]

Lenin understood the need for alliances with the peasants and the non-Russians, and he was convinced that the approaching international socialist revolution would make the movements for land and statehood largely irrelevant. Acutely aware that the weakness of the central state gave new potency to movements for autonomy and separation from the empire, as well as the spontaneous resolution of the land question by peasants, Lenin staked out a clear position supporting both processes. In contrast, neither the Provisional Government nor the successive White leaderships were sympathetic to the nationalists.

Immediately after taking power, the Bolsheviks set up the People's Commissariat of Nationalities under Stalin and issued a series of declarations on "the rights of the toiling and exploited peoples," "to all Muslim toilers of Russia and the East," and on the disposition of Turkish Armenia. Most importantly, with little real ability to effect its will in the peripheries, the Soviet government made a strategic shift in response to the growing number of autonomies and accepted by January 1918 the principle of federalism. As they launched an attack on Ukraine, the Bolsheviks announced that they recognized the Central Executive Committee of Soviets of Ukraine as "the supreme authority in Ukraine" and accepted "a federal union with Russia and complete unity in matters of internal and external policy." By the end of the month, the Third Congress of Soviets resolved: "The Soviet Russian Republic is established on the basis of a free union of free nations, as a federation of Soviet national republics."

Both federalism and national-territorial autonomy were written into the first Soviet constitution, adopted in July 1918. As Richard Pipes has noted, "Soviet Russia . . . became the first modern state to place the national principle at the base of its federal structure."[4]

In the ferocity of the civil war, many Communists, particularly those in the peripheries or of non-Russian origin, opposed Lenin's principled stand in favor of national self-determination, fearing the dissolution of the unitary state. As early as December 1917, Stalin argued that the freedom of self-determination should be given only to the laboring classes, not to the bourgeoisie. At the Eighth Party Congress in March 1919, Bukharin supported Stalin's position and tried to divide the national from the colonial question. Only in those nations where the proletariat had not defined its interests as separate from the bourgeoisie should the slogan of "self-determination of nations" be employed. Lenin's formula, he claimed, was appropriate only "for Hottentots, Bushmen, Negroes, Indians," whereas Stalin's notion of "self-determination for the laboring classes" corresponded to the period in which the dictatorship of the proletariat was being established.[5]

Lenin answered Bukharin sharply. "There are no Bushmen in Russia; as for the Hottentots, I also have not heard that they have pretensions to an autonomous republic, but we have the Bashkirs, the Kyrgyz, a whole series of other peoples, and in relation to them we cannot refuse recognition." All nations, he reasserted, have the right to self-determination, and Bolshevik support for this principle would aid the self-determination of the laboring classes. The stage of a given nation as it moved from "medieval forms to bourgeois democracy and on to proletarian democracy" should be considered, he stated, but it was difficult to differentiate the interests of the proletariat and the bourgeoisie, which had been sharply defined only in Russia.[6]

The final resolution of the Congress was a compromise between Lenin's tolerance of nationalism and the more militant opposition to it. Maintaining the principle of national self-determination, the resolution went on to say: "As to the question who is the carrier of the nation's will to separation, the RKP stands on the historico-class point-of-view, taking into consideration the level of historical development on which a given nation stands."[7] The Bolsheviks reached no consensus on nationality policy, and the conflict between those who, like Lenin, considered the national agenda of non-Russians and those who, like Stalin, subordinated the national to the "proletarian" continued until the former's death and the latter's consolidation of power within the party. On the ground, Communists decided themselves who was the carrier of the nation's will, and after the initial recognition of independence for Finland, Poland, the Baltic republics, and (for a time) Georgia, few other gestures were made toward "separatists."

Toward the end of 1919, while reflecting on the factors that had led to Bolshevik victory in 1917, Lenin turned to Ukraine to underscore the importance of tolerance in national policy. Reviewing the Constituent Assembly election results, in which Ukrainian SRs and socialists outpolled the Russian SRs, he noted: "The division between the Russian and Ukrainian Socialist Revolutionaries as early as 1917 could not have been accidental." Without holding that national sentiments are fixed or permanent, he suggested once again that internationalists must be tolerant of the changing national consciousness of non-Russians, which, he was confident, was part of the petty bourgeois vacillation that had been characteristic of the peasantry throughout the civil war.

> The question whether the Ukraine will be a separate state is far less important [than the fundamental interests of the proletarian dictatorship, the unity of the Red Army, or the leading role of the proletariat in relation to the peasantry]. We must not be in the least surprised, or frightened, even by the prospect of the

Ukrainian workers and peasants trying out different systems, and in the course of, say, several years, testing by practice union with the RSFSR, or seceding from the latter and forming an independent Ukrainian SSR, or various forms of their close alliance. . . .

The vacillation of non-proletarian working people on *such* a question is quite natural, even inevitable, but not in the least frightful for the proletariat. It is the duty of the proletarian who is really capable of being an internationalist . . . to leave it to the non-proletarian masses *themselves* to *get rid* of this vacillation as a result of their own experience.[8]

As the strategic situation improved for the Bolsheviks and their allies by the summer of 1920, the "national-colonial question" was put squarely on the agenda. The British were leaving the Russian periphery, and communism had gained its first foothold south of the Caucasus with the relatively easy Sovietization of Azerbaijan in April. The balance of forces in Central Asia and in Transcaucasia, where Georgia and Armenia remained independent, was clearly in favor of the Soviets, and direct links were established between the Soviets and the Kemalist nationalists in Anatolia. On April 26, Kemal sent an official communication to Moscow expressing his appreciation of Moscow's fight against imperialism and his readiness to take upon himself "military operations against the imperialist Armenian government" and to encourage Azerbaijan "to enter the Bolshevik state union."[9] In May, Soviet troops and the Persian revolutionary Kuchuk Khan established the Soviet republic of Gilan on the southern coast of the Caspian Sea, and though the situation in Persia remained extraordinarily fluid, the government at Teheran appeared prepared to distance itself from the British and open negotiations with the Soviets. With Denikin defeated, Kolchak dead, and the Red Army marching against Pilsudski's Poland, the latter half of 1920 turned out to be a high point of revolutionary enthusiasm and direct Bolshevik promotion of the revolution in the East.

Several themes repeatedly reasserted themselves in the

discussions around the national-colonial question in 1920, both at the Second Congress of the Communist International and the Baku Congress of the Peoples of the East. The first was Lenin's leitmotiv, which had haunted his writings since 1914—the relationship of capitalist imperialism and the revolutionary crisis in both the advanced and the colonial world. Besides the one billion people living in colonial and semicolonial states, and another quarter-billion living in Russia, since the war Germany, Austria, and Bulgaria, he argued, had been relegated to "what amounts to colonial status." The "super-profits of thousands of millions form the economic basis on which opportunism in the labour movement is built."[10] This dependency of the capitalist metropole on the colonial and semicolonial world was recognized by all communists, but some non-European communists, like the Indian M. N. Roy and "many comrades in Turkestan" (referred to by the Iranian delegate Sultan Zade at the Second World Congress), went further and argued that the revolution in Europe required a revolution in the East.

A second theme was the failure of the Second International to address the colonial issue in a revolutionary manner. Lenin, Roy, Sultan Zade, and others portrayed the Social Democrats as Eurocentric reformers, willing to support movements toward self-government in the colonies but reluctant to back revolutionary efforts. Communists, on the other hand, recognized the need for collaboration between revolutionaries in Europe, America, and Asia, and took pride in the multiracial representation in the Comintern meetings.

A third dominant theme was the historic difference between bourgeois democracy, supported by the Social Democrats of Europe, and soviet democracy, and the strong sense that a new historical epoch had opened that had rendered parliamentarianism obsolete.[11] In his "Preliminary Theses on the National-Colonial Question," Lenin began with the distinction between formal bourgeois democracy, which grants juridical equality to all, and "the real meaning of the demand of equality," which requires the abolition of classes.[12] Bourgeois democracy also disguised the exploitation of weaker nations by the stronger, though the imperialist war of 1914–18 had exposed this hypocrisy. Only a common struggle of all proletarians and laboring people of all nations could overthrow the rule of the landlords and bourgeoisie.

Yet another theme was the nature of the future socialist state, a grand multinational federation not unlike the Russian Socialist Federative Soviet Republic (RSFSR). Federation, Lenin maintained, was the advanced form for the full unity of the toilers of different countries. Federation already had shown its utility in practice, both in the relations of the RSFSR with other soviet republics (Hungarian, Finnish, and Latvian in the past; Azerbaijani and Ukrainian in the present) and, within the RSFSR, in relations with the nationalities that earlier had not had either state existence or autonomy (for example, the Bashkir and Tatar autonomous republics in the RSFSR). It was essential to work for a tighter federative union, both politically and economically, but at the same time, Lenin cautioned, full recognition of the rights of nations and minorities, including the right to separate states, had to be supported.

Differences in tone and direction arose in discussions of appropriate strategies to win over the masses of the East. In his original theses delivered to the Second Comintern Congress, Lenin had argued that "all communist parties must aid the bourgeois-democratic liberation movement" in backward countries with feudal or patriarchal relations. While fighting against clerical reaction and medieval elements, against Pan-Islam and other movements that attempt to unite the liberation movement while strengthening the khans, landlords, mullahs, etc., communists must support the peasant movement against landlords by forming a "provisional alliance" with bourgeois democracy of the colonies and backward countries.

When Lenin submitted his theses to his comrades, he met resistance to his provisional alliance with the national bourgeoisie. Lenin assured the doubters that "the alliance with the peasantry is more strongly underlined for me (and this is not completely equal to the bourgeoisie)."[13] Most vociferously, Roy disputed Lenin's support of the national bourgeoisie and argued that Lenin was mistaken to believe that the national liberation movement had the significance of the bourgeois democratic revolution. Though as yet an unproven revolutionary, Roy (as he tells us in his memoirs)

> pointed out that the bourgeoisie even in the most advanced colonial countries, like India, as a class, was not economically and culturally differentiated from the feudal social order: therefore, the nationalist movement was ideologically reactionary in the sense that the triumph would not necessarily mean a bourgeois democratic revolution. The role of Gandhi was the crucial point of difference. Lenin believed that, as the inspirer and leader of a mass movement, he was a revolutionary. I maintained that, as a religious and cultural revivalist, he was bound to be a reactionary socially, however revolutionary he might appear politically.[14]

After several private discussions with Roy and a general debate in the Commission on the National-Colonial Question, Lenin admitted that his views had been changed by Roy's challenge.[15] Roy argued that

> foreign domination constantly obstructs the free development of social life; therefore the revolution's first step must be the removal of this foreign domination. The struggle to overthrow foreign domination in the colonies does not therefore mean underwriting the national aims of the national bourgeoisie but much rather smoothing the path to liberation for the proletariat of the colonies.

Roy distinguished more clearly than Lenin the two opposing movements in the colonial world: "the bourgeois-democratic nationalist movement, which pursues the program of political liberation with the conservation of the capitalist order; [and] the struggle of the propertyless peasants for their liberation from every kind of exploitation."[16] Communists must not allow the former movement to dominate the latter and must ally with and support the latter. Lenin agreed that Communists should support "national-revolutionary" movements but withhold support from reformist movements based on collaboration of the colonial and the metropolitan bourgeoisies. In the absence of a proletariat, as in Turkestan, the Communist party must take over the leading role "in order to awaken independent political thinking and political action."[17]

Though he held on to his principle of national self-determination, Lenin's adjustment to Roy's formulation had a political effect similar to the move by Stalin and Bukharin to consider the stage that a nation had reached. Both undermined the authenticity of the claims of nationalism and removed the restraints that Lenin had previously proposed. These more revolutionary positions pushed the Communists to a leadership in the peripheral and colonial struggles that hardly corresponded to their real power in these regions. In the absence of a significant proletariat, in situations where the only viable revolutionary movement was one that Communists could not bring themselves to support wholly, the party became a surrogate proletariat. Instead of being engaged in the actual revolution, which was anticolonial and led by nationalists or ethnosocialists, the party constructed a reading of the political moment that allowed them extraordinary freedom and left them open to precisely the charges of Russian expansionism of which Lenin had warned.

Within a few months, the Armenian republic, facing an invasion by the Kemalist Turks, capitulated to the Bolshevik forces stationed on its border as the lesser evil. In February 1921, the Red Army drove the Mensheviks out of Georgia.

Both Transcaucasian "revolutions" were far more artificial and external than had been the collapse of Azerbaijan, where Bolsheviks enjoyed considerable support from Baku workers. Though at first the Armenian Communists agreed to work with the Dashnaks and Lenin preferred some accommodation with the Georgian Mensheviks, in both cases the moderates were quickly eliminated and purely Communist political orders were established. In Transcaucasia, at least, no real attempt was made to implement the more cautious aspect of Comintern strategy, namely, limited cooperation with non-Communist nationalists. Rather, the more militant reading of that strategy, advancing as soon as possible to Communist direction of the movement, was adopted. But in Armenia and Georgia, where there was no significant support for Bolshevism, the party remained an isolated political force until time, inertia, and coercion brought grudging acquiescence from the population.

The first phase of the Comintern's involvement with the peoples of the East was over by late 1921. The revolutionary wave had receded, and the Soviet government began to see itself as one state among many, albeit with a different historical role. The link between the national question within the USSR and the anti-imperialist struggle abroad became more tenuous. Perhaps most ominously, in the light of a resistant reality in which the inevitable movement toward communism appeared stalled, the gap widened between the actual practice of Bolsheviks and the inflated rhetoric that disguised it.

Bolsheviks were a minority party representing a social class that had nearly disappeared in the civil war. With no political or cultural hegemony over the vast peasant masses and with exceptional vulnerability in the non-Russian regions, the Communist parties moderated their own leap into socialism. The years of the New Economic Policy (1921–28) were a period of strategic compromise with the peasantry in both Russia and the national republics, a time of retreat and patience awaiting the delayed international revolution. Lenin continued to advocate caution and sensitivity toward non-Russians, whereas many of his comrades, most notably Stalin and Orjonikidze, were less willing to accommodate even moderate nationalists. In several republics, leaders of defeated parties were quickly removed from power and driven into exile; but other former members of the nationalist or moderate socialist movements were integrated into the Communist parties and state apparatus. The Bolshevik project now involved the building of a new federated state that would both nurture the nations within it and forge new loyalties to the ideals of the socialists.

Nations and States

Though in popular understanding and in nationalists' ideologies the nation is usually thought to exist prior to the state and to be the basis on which the state has been formed, historians have long recognized the importance of states in the creation of nations. A quarter-century ago, Victor Kiernan wrote: "Of the two elements (nation-state) included here, it was the state that came first and fashioned the mould for the nation." The process by which the new state created the conditions for turning "a vague sense of nationality . . . into conscious nationalism" was intimately linked with the new (Renaissance) monarchies' relationship to the constituent social classes and their struggles.[18] Ernest Gellner places the state at the center of his theory of nationalism, along with industrial society, and declares bluntly that "the problem of nationalism does not arise from stateless societies."[19] Likewise, in a recent critique of John Breuilly's work on nationalism and the state, Henry Patterson agrees that "in the transition from some sense of cultural or ethnic identity to full-blown nationalism the development of the state is crucial."[20] He faults Breuilly for neglecting the ways nationalisms build on class coalitions and argues that the very success of nationalist movements, which are always class coalitions with ostensibly classless ideologies, requires an "approach that allows for the crucial role of the framework of state institutions in providing a point for the constitution and focusing of nationalist objectives."[21]

On the empirical level, the centrality of the state in nation formation has been exhaustively elaborated in an influential book by Eugen Weber, *Peasants into Frenchmen*: he shows how for a great number of French peasants a sense of being French overcame more local and particularistic identities only a century after the French Revolution.[22] Here the state was fundamental in establishing a unified school system with a homogeneous French language, mobilizing men into an army that socialized them to new norms, and breaking down the cultural and social isolation of thousands of villages. On the other hand, although it is evident that state policies and interstate warfare create opportunities for consolidating nationality and nation, it is equally clear that the original exemplars of nation-states, England and France, however they may have been formed, had a relatively homogeneous ethnic core around which other ethnic groups consolidated. The ideal for nationalists, which then was read back into the past as if it were "real history," was the coincidence of state with pre-existing nationality. With the emergence of the democratic discourse of national self-determination, it was only a small step to conclude that the only (or at least, the most) legitimate states were those based on the "natural" affinities offered by ethnicity.

"Making of Nations," Soviet-Style

The making of nationality and the spread of nationalism involved political conjunctures in which people were forced

to make less ambiguous choices about their friends and enemies than they had in the past. However artificial the generation of the independent republics that mushroomed in
the turned-up soil of the revolution, the very experience of a
brief statehood had a profound influence on future developments. The years of independence, the ascendancy of a more
nationalist discourse among their intelligentsias, and the
involuntary Sovietization all contributed to the growth of
secular nationalist sentiments. But the displacement of populations, the forced migration of much of the old nationalist
intelligentsia and bourgeoisie, and the vast devastation of
the economy, particularly in cities, during the civil war provided a political opportunity for the Bolsheviks, who proposed a program of recovery and limited self-determination.

The experience of independence and intervention differed
greatly from nationality to nationality. Among the most
successful was the Georgian republic, often cited as a model
of a Social Democratic peasant republic by Western enthu-
siasts; it managed to defend itself against threats from the
White forces under Denikin, rebellious local minorities, and
Armenian incursions before it succumbed to the invading
Red Army. In both Georgia and Armenia, parliamentary systems with representation of oppositional parties were imple-
mented, and in both republics, desperate revolts by Mensheviks and Dashnaks after the establishment of Soviet power
testified to continuing support for the anti-Soviet leaderships.

The picture is far less clear elsewhere in the non-Russian
peripheries. In Ukraine, the destructiveness of the civil war
(in which an estimated one million Ukrainians died), the
fragility of each of the established governments, and the
ferocity of the terror on both sides left a society devastated
and desperate for peaceful recovery. The dearth of social
historical research on the revolution in Ukraine prevents
firm conclusions about the success of nationalist mobilization. The years of civil war were marked by political frag-

mentation and localism. Villagers turned inward in both
psychological and physical self-defense. Though it is difficult to follow the extreme conclusion that the "raising of
national consciousness of the peasantry, which began in
1917, was completed by the peasants' experience of the various Soviet regimes, foreign intervention as well as Denikin's occupation of Ukraine," Ukrainian nationalism was far
stronger and more widespread at the end of the civil war
than at the beginning.[23] Identification with a territorial nation would grow even more impressively in the 1920s under
Soviet rule.[24]

In the lands inhabited by the Kazakhs, a fierce triangular
struggle pitted urban-based Bolsheviks against local White
forces and the Kazakh Alash Orda autonomous movement.
As they fought alongside the Whites between 1918 and 1919,
Alash Orda grew discontented with Kolchak's resistance to
their autonomy and attempted to negotiate with Moscow.
With the defeat of the Whites late in 1919, the Bolsheviks
tried to win over the Kazakhs through a broad amnesty and
concessions to local autonomy. In the absence of alternatives, Kazakhs acquiesced to Bolshevik rule. They returned
to their seminomadic mode of existence and regenerated
their traditional social structures in the new guise of local
soviet power.[25]

For those who ended up outside the Soviet federation, like
the Baltic peoples, the even longer independence period and
the brutality with which it was ended helped to define their
representation of nation. The political and economic power
of the Baltic German elites was eliminated in the early years
of independence, and, though minority cultures were permitted free expression, the dominant nationalities now promoted their own ethnic cultural and educational institutions. Demographically the Baltic republics were securely
national. In the 1922 census, Estonians made up 87.6 percent of the republic's population; according to 1935 figures,

Latvians comprised 75.5 percent of their state's population; and in 1937, Lithuanians made up 84.2 percent of the population in their republic.[26] The parliamentary systems established in all three republics in the revolutionary period succumbed to more dictatorial forms in the late 1920s and 1930s, and hostility between the Baltic republics and their Soviet neighbor increased in the years before World War II. Yet for all their political and economic difficulties, the Baltic states demonstrated viability as independent political actors, and the memory of that experience remained for the half-century of Soviet rule after 1940, eventually mobilizing the Baltic peoples in the Gorbachev years.

In the nationalist discourses of the present movements for self-determination in the Soviet Union, the brief period of independence has been transformed into a moment of light to contrast with the long, dark experience with Soviet rule, which in turn is depicted as the destruction of the national. Repression, forced Russification, imposed modernization, the suppression of national traditions, the destruction of the village, even an assault on nature are combined in powerful images that show Soviet power as the enemy of the nation. Lost in this powerful nationalist rhetoric is any sense of the degree to which the long and difficult years of Communist party rule actually continued the "making of nations" of the prerevolutionary period. As the present generation watches the self-destruction of the Soviet Union, the irony is lost that the USSR was the victim not only of its negative effects on the non-Russian peoples but of its own "progressive" contribution to the process of nation-building.

The first state in history to be formed of ethnic political units, the USSR was a pseudofederal state that both eliminated political sovereignty for the nationalities and guaranteed them territorial identity, educational and cultural institutions in their own language, and the promotion of native cadres into positions of power. Though the powerful appeal of nationalism has been a global phenomenon in the twentieth century, its potency in the Soviet Union requires analysis of the peculiar historic formation of coherent, conscious nations in a unique political system that deliberately set out to thwart nationalism. At least seven fundamental trends over the seven decades of Soviet power can be explored to provide the context in which mass ethnic nationalisms exploded in the 1980s. We shall look in turn at nativization, economic and social transformation, territorialization, imperialism, traditionalism, localism, and national mobilization.

Nativization

The policy of "nativization" (*korenizatsiia*), encouraged by Lenin and supported by Stalin until the early 1930s, contributed to the consolidation of nationality in three important ways: by supporting the native language, by creating a national intelligentsia and political elite, and by formally institutionalizing ethnicity in the state apparatus.

Already in the years of civil war, the Soviet governments adopted laws establishing the equality of languages in courts and administration, the free choice of language in schooling, and the protection of minority languages. The short-lived Latvian Soviet government adopted such a law as early as January 1918, as did the Ukrainian Soviet authorities in December 1919. In Belorussia, four different languages—Belorussian, Russian, Polish, and Yiddish—were used in signs, in local governments, and in schools. The central state promoted alphabets for peoples who had no writing, opened schools for those who had had none under tsarism, and set up hundreds of national soviets for peoples living outside their national regions. In ways strikingly similar to the work of patriotic intellectuals on behalf of some nationalities in the nineteenth century, Soviet activists set out to create educational systems and literary languages for their peoples by selecting the dialect to be promoted and by systematizing, refining, and "purifying" the lexicon.[27] By 1927, 82 percent of the schools in Ukraine had been Ukrainized, and more than three-quarters of the pupils were attending Ukrainian-language schools.[28]

Russian officials were steadily replaced by national leaders, and since many of the new Bolshevik cadres in the national republics were former members of other parties, like the Ukrainian Left SRs (known as *Borotbisti* [Fighters]), the nativization campaigns created a broad base of support for the common enterprise of ethnic liberation and socialist construction. The formation of new political classes in the national republics, Communist but made up of the local nationality, can be observed from figures for membership in the Communist parties. In 1922, 72 percent of all Communists were Russians; only 15,000 were from traditionally Muslim peoples (6,534 Tatars, 4,964 Kazakhs). Five years later, Russians made up only 65 percent of the RKP(b), and the various national regions of the USSR—union republics, autonomous republics and regions, and national territories—had achieved a level of 46.6 percent native membership (about 180,000 Communists). This trend continued until about 1932, when the native Communist party membership in the national regions reached 53.8 percent (582,000 Communists).[29] Ukrainian membership in the Ukrainian Communist party increased from 24 percent to 59 percent in the decade 1922–32; Belorussians grew from 21 percent to 60 percent of the Belorussian party. In Transcaucasia, meanwhile, the already high native percentages grew at a less spectacular rate: in Georgia, from 62 percent to 66 percent; in Armenia, from 89 percent to 90 percent; in Azerbaijan, from 39 percent to 44 percent. The figures for Central Asia were particularly noteworthy: Kazakh membership in the republican Communist party grew from 8 percent to 53 percent (1924–33), and every party in the region (that reported figures) had a majority of native members.[30]

A similar trend can be observed in the state apparatuses of the Union republics, though here the representation of the local nationalities was far greater at the *raion* (district) level than at the republic level. In Ukraine in 1929, for example, Ukrainians made up 36 percent of the apparatus at the republic level and 76 percent at the *raion* level. The corresponding figures for Belorussians were 49.5 percent and 73 percent; for Azerbaijanis, 36 percent and 69 percent; for Georgians, 74 percent and 81 percent; for Armenians, 93.5 percent and 94.6 percent; for Turkmen, 8.4 percent and 24 percent; for Uzbeks, 11.5 percent and 41.6 percent; and for Tajiks, 14 percent and 45 percent.[31]

But the policy of nativization was contested by party members suspicious of concessions to nationality and of the inclusion in the party and state of peoples less committed to the rigid vision of the dominant faction in the Communist party. Stalin and his closest comrades were particularly hostile to the growth of "national communisms" in Georgia and Ukraine, and a bitter confrontation over the extent to which autonomy should be allowed in the non-Russian republics cooled relations between Stalin and the ailing Lenin. Once Lenin had been incapacitated by a series of strokes, Stalin used his power to exile to diplomatic posts both the Georgian Bolshevik Budu Mdivani and one of the early leaders of Ukraine, the Bulgarian Khristian Rakovskii.[32] To Stalin, local nationalism appeared to be a greater danger than the Great Russian Chauvinism of which Lenin repeatedly warned.

Despite opposition from strategically located opponents and countervailing tendencies toward political centralization, the nativization policies bore a rich harvest in the 1920s, as works by Zvi Gitelman, Bohdan Krawchenko, James Mace, and George Liber attest.[33] In Armenia, the Communists spoke of the resurrection of Armenia from the ashes of genocide, and although they drove out or arrested the anti-Bolshevik nationalists, they began the rebuilding of an Armenian state to which refugees from other parts of the Soviet Union and the world could migrate. The cosmopolitan capitals of Georgia and Azerbaijan now became the seats of power of native Communists, and the infrastructures of national states, complete with national operas, national academies of science, and national film studios, were built up.

In each of the national republics, national identity was both transformed and reinforced in its new form. In Ukraine, for example, where in prerevolutionary times Ukrainian peasants had easily assimilated to a Russified working class, the new political environment and the shifts in national awareness in the 1920s were reflected in the increase in the number of "Ukrainians" in towns. "There were two aspects to this process," writes Bohdan Krawchenko. "The first was the re-absorption into a Ukrainian identity of assimilated Ukrainians. The second was that Russification, if not halted, was certainly reduced to a minimum. This meant that assimilation did not offset whatever gains Ukrainians made by urban immigration."[34] Ukrainians and other non-Russian peoples gained an urban presence they had never enjoyed before, and the dominance of Russians in the cities was compromised. "We will not forcibly Ukrainise the Russian proletariat in Ukraine," said a Ukrainian Communist leader, "but we will ensure that the Ukrainian . . . when he goes to the city will not be Russified . . . and yes, we will repaint the signs in towns."[35]

Even after it was undercut by the Stalinist emphasis on rapid industrialization, the Soviet policy of *korenizatsiia*, which involved the promotion of national languages and national cadres in the governance of national areas, increased the language capabilities and the politicization of the non-Russians in the national republics. The creation of national working classes, newly urbanized populations, national intelligentsias, and ethnic political elites contributed to the more complete elaboration of nationhood.

Yet even as ethnicity was being strengthened in some ways, it was being limited and even undermined in others. Official Soviet doctrine repeated Lenin's prediction of *sblizhenie* (rapprochement) and *sliianie* (merger) of Soviet peoples and of the creation of a single Soviet culture. Mobility, acculturation of political and intellectual elites, the preference for Russian schooling, and the generalized effects of industrialization and urbanization created anxiety about assimilation and loss of culture. A deep contradiction developed: on the one hand, *korenizatsiia* and the "renationalization" of ethnic groups in the Soviet years created strong nationalist pressures; on the other, state policies transformed an agrarian society into an industrial urban one and promoted assimilation to a generalized Soviet culture.

Economic and Social Transformation

The policy of nativization was invoked simultaneously with a Soviet program of economic development and social transformation. In the 1920s, both the restoration of the devastated economy and the rooting of Soviet power in the Russian countryside and the non-Russian republics were carried out in the context of *korenizatsiia* and the moderate mixed economy of the New Economic Policy. But in the period of the greatest acceleration of industrialization and urbanization, when the entire economy of the Soviet Union was transformed from a mixed state and market economy into a highly centralized command economy, the cultural and political impulses of "national communism" and the imperatives of Stalin's "revolution-from-above" were irreconcilably polarized. As Stalin moved to consolidate his power in the early 1930s, ethnic interests were subordinated to considerations of economic efficiency. Centralization and the radical decrease of republic autonomy coincided with a major shift in nationality policy. *Korenizatsiia*, though never officially rejected, was steadily replaced by antinationalistic campaigns. Most dramatically, in Ukraine, the Postyshev government viciously attacked the Ukrainizers and criticized their promotion of Ukrainian education and culture. A powerful Ukrainian national Communist, Commissar of Education Mykola Skypnyk, killed himself on July 7, 1933. Half a year later, Stalin himself signaled the turn against *korenizatsiia* when he amended Lenin's assertion that Great Russian Chauvinism was a greater danger than small-nation nationalism. The greatest danger, the proletarian dictator declared, comes from the nationalism that one has forgotten to combat.[36]

The collectivization of agriculture, resisted by hundreds of thousands of peasants, devastated the traditionally patriarchal village leaderships and subjugated what had been an independent peasantry to the dictates of state officials. In Ukraine, the imposed targets for the grain collections far exceeded the peasantry's production capability, and once the reserves and even seed grain were exhausted, a massive famine resulted that left millions dead.[37] In Kazakhstan, collectivization was combined with forcible settlement of nomads, and Kazakhs responded by destroying 80 percent of their herds. Hundreds of thousands migrated, and millions died from violence and starvation.[38] Throughout the Soviet Union, collectivization and attacks on local nationalism coincided with campaigns against the Church and the Mosque. In Azerbaijan and Central Asia, women were compelled to give up the veil. In Armenia, the head of the national church was murdered. Thousands of churches, mosques, and synagogues were closed or destroyed.

Simultaneously, rapid, forced industrialization resulted in social and geographical mobility that further disrupted traditional patterns of authority and cultural practices. A new working class drafted from the peasantry appeared in towns and at new factory sites, without industrial skills, ignorant of labor traditions and organizations, and subject to a rising elite of managers and technicians, themselves vulnerable to those still higher up. By the mid-1930s, cadres were chosen more for their technical abilities or loyalty to the General Line than for their ethnic (or even class) background.

To succeed, a party official or economic manager had to be literate in the general Russian culture of the elite. Reflecting the Russophilia of the dictator, Stalinism promoted the Russian language and culture. By the end of the 1930s, Russian-language study was compulsory in all schools. Though native languages were also taught, their status was inferior to the all-state language, Russian, and they were often seen as insufficient for successful careers in politics or science.

By 1946, the Russian membership of the all-union Communist party had risen to 67.8 percent, and native membership in the national regions had fallen to 45 percent.[39] The extreme centralization of Stalin's autocracy made any manifestation of local autonomy a criminal act. A whole generation of national Communist leaders, many of them the founders of the parties in the non-Russian republics, were physically eliminated in the Great Terror of the late 1930s. By the outbreak of World War II, Stalin's absolute power meant the absolute powerlessness of all peoples and their elites in the USSR. His own whims and suspicions soon led him to the most reckless and arbitrary treatment of the non-Russians, even to the abolition of several autonomous republics and regions and the exiling of whole peoples from their homelands to Siberia or Central Asia.[40]

The contradictory Soviet policies of *korenizatsiia* and economic and social transformation had different effects both within nationalities and among different peoples. Many nationalities underwent internal consolidation and a growth of national consciousness, whereas others suffered more extremely from state-enforced Russification. In Belorussia, for example, there were no Belorussian schools available in cities by the 1970s; Armenians and Georgians, on the other hand, felt few effects though they often complained bitterly about the imposition of a bilingual policy. Several nationalities, notably the Kazakhs, Estonians, and Latvians, were weakened demographically by the in-migration of Russians and other Slavs, often as industrial workers and technicians, though others, like the Armenians, Azerbaijanis, and Georgians, increased their percentages in the republics' population. Estonians and Georgians vigorously resisted learning Russian and defended native-language use, whereas hundreds of thousands of Ukrainians lost the ability to communicate with ease in the language of their grandparents.

Though the industrialization, urbanization, and greater social mobility associated with Soviet programs of development acculturated many non-Russians to a homogenized Soviet way of life, they did not obliterate ethnic identity or assimilate non-Russians totally in an ethnic Russian culture. The official policy of bringing the Soviet peoples together had registered enviable success by the Brezhnev period. By 1979, 62.2 percent of non-Russians considered themselves fluent in Russian.[41] On the other hand, despite the brutal reversals in the nativization policies of the 1920s and the promotion of Russian language and culture under Stalin, the processes set in motion by *korenizatsiia* continued until, by the 1960s, most of the republics had become more national in character, not only demographically, but politically and culturally as well. What were in effect "affirmative-action programs" promoted cadres from the titular nationalities, often to the detriment of the more urbanized and educated Russian (and in Azerbaijan and Georgia, Armenian) population.[42] Education remained national, though secularized and "socialist in content"; national languages were taught, but whereas Russian was compulsory for non-Russians, after 1958 learning the language of the republic in which one lived was not obligatory.

Territorialization

Related to the process of nativization during the Soviet period was the territorialization of ethnicity. Formerly, many ethnic and religious communities had much greater loyalty to and identity with either the area in which they lived or, in the case of many Muslims, the worldwide Islamic community (the *'umma*). Supranational and subnational loyalties competed with the more specifically national ones.[43] For certain ethnicities, most notably those of Central Asia, the establishment of territorial administrative units on the basis of nationality in the early 1920s was unprecedented and provided clear political and territorial identities as alternatives to earlier religious and tribal solidarities. Following Stalin's own definition of nation, Soviet authorities promoted an idea of nation fixed to territory.

Migration strengthened the titular nationalities in many republics, consolidating the identity of ethnicity with territory. In the centuries before the revolution, the Russian empire had been a place of constant migration, with tribes and peoples moving from one area to another. In Transcaucasia, for example, after the Russo-Persian and Russo-Turkish wars, Muslims left for the empires to the south and Armenians migrated north into Erevan province, to Tbilisi (Tiflis) and Baku. The population of towns was mixed, with Armenians being the most urbanized of the three peoples, but in the Soviet period high rates of urbanization led to solid majorities of Azerbaijanis in Baku and of Georgians in Tbilisi. Yet even as ethnic consolidation rose, anomalous enclaves of ethnic minorities remained: in Mountainous Karabagh, an autonomous region in Azerbaijan, over three-quarters of the population was Armenian; in Abkhazia, an autonomous republic in Georgia, the Abkhaz minority was threatened by the growing Georgian plurality. Dozens of Azerbaijani villages remained in Georgia and Armenia, whereas Armenian and Georgian villages could be found in Azerbaijan.

With the coming of Soviet power, cosmopolitanism declined, except in parts of the RSFSR and the Baltic republics, and many formerly multinational regions and cities gradually became more ethnically homogeneous. Tbilisi, a city that had been dominated by Armenians and Russians both demographically and politically before the revolution, first achieved a Georgian majority in the 1960s. Baku steadily became Azerbaijani in the Soviet period, though Armenians and Russians remained in middle-level positions of authority. But in the aftermath of the Karabagh conflict, Azerbaijanis stormed through the streets of Baku in January 1990, killing Armenians and forcing the survivors to flee from the city under Russian protection. Erevan, which as a small town in the late nineteenth century still contained a large Muslim population, grew into a nearly purely Armenian city through the in-migration of Armenians from other parts of the Soviet Union and the Armenian diaspora.

The territorialization of ethnicity and the increased power of the titular nationality created new problems of national minorities and diasporas, peoples with few guarantees or means of redress for their accumulating grievances. The legacies of empire were not uniform. They left some republics more demographically compact and others less homogeneous. After seventy years of Soviet power, about sixty million Soviet citizens lived outside of their (or had no) "homeland." Twenty-five million of these dispersed people considered themselves Russian.

The Soviet empire had created territorial nations, with their own state apparatuses and ruling elites. Each had the trappings of any sovereign state, from the national opera house to a national flag and seal, but without real sovereignty or the right to full political expression. What Tom Nairn calls a "reservation culture" had been established: ethnolinguistic culture without political nationalism was the only permissible, "healthy" nationhood.[44]

Imperialism

Relations between the center and the ethnic peripheries remained basically imperial, that is, inequitable and based on a subordinate relationship to the Russian center. After the revolution, these relationships were disguised and justified by reference to a supranational ideology and a compelling vision of history that sanctioned the rule of the Communist party. In a Russocentric empire, in which Russian was most closely identified with Soviet, proletarian, and progress, ethnicity conferred both relative advantage and relative disadvantage. As a fundamental marker of official identity, ethnicity made people eligible for either promotion and access to privileges (if, for example, they were members of the titular nationality of a given republic) or discrimination (if they were not). In certain contexts, even being Russian could be a disadvantage, and being Jewish increasingly became a liability in the years following World War II. Stalin's "anticosmopolitan" campaigns were virulently anti-Semitic, culminating in the frameup of the infamous "Doctors' Plot" of the early 1950s; but even in the post-Stalin period, milder forms of anti-Semitism were rampant in party circles and were manifest in promotion policies, admission quotas for higher education, and the very definition of what constituted extralegal dissent.

Native cadres may have governed in Azerbaijan or Uzbekistan (particularly after the 1920s, when native Communists were few), but policies were largely determined in Moscow, and local interests were subordinated to all-Union goals. Non-Russian republics were treated as objects of central

policy rather than as subjects capable of independent deci-
sion-making, and their national destinies were fundamentally altered as a result. In Kazakhstan, for example, where
the imposition of collectivization of agriculture resulted in
the loss of 40 percent of the population through either death
or migration, the nomadic population was forcibly settled
on the land, fundamentally changing its ancient way of
life. Industrial and agricultural development, particularly
Khrushchev's Virgin Lands program of the 1950s, resulted in
the settlement of non-Kazakhs in the republic, until by 1979
Kazakhs made up only 33 percent of the republic's population.
Moreover, Kazakhstan was used as a test area for atomic
weapons and a way station for up-and-coming party leaders
like Leonid Brezhnev, who served as party chief briefly in
1955–56.[45]

A fundamental contradiction between empire and emerging nations grew like a cancer within the Soviet state.
Much more than the tsarist empire, the USSR had become a
"prisonhouse of nations"—indeed, of nations that had grown
up within the Soviet Union. The inherently inequitable political relations between the center and the republics (and
within republics, between the capital and the autonomies)
became increasingly intolerable as nationalities became capable of self-development. By the post-Stalin period, both
titular nationalities in the union republics and minorities
within republics expressed growing frustration at restraints
on development imposed by bureaucratic centralism.

Traditionalism

For all the transformative effects of Soviet-style economic
and social development, traditional cultural practices and
social structures persisted. What Massell calls "the old uni-
ties based on kinship, custom, and belief" managed to survive even as traditional leaderships were removed, religion

was officially undermined, and the social environment was fundamentally changed.[46] In Central Asia, for example, the patriarchal forms of female subjugation proved resistant to efforts by the party to liberate women. The lack of a native proletariat and of clearly delineated class lines led the regime in the 1920s to attempt to use women as a "surrogate proletariat," an improvised "class" wedge to force cleavages in traditional Muslim societies. Women were encouraged to take off their veils, seek work outside the household, and challenge the patriarchal authority of their fathers and brothers. The experiment, which resulted in beatings and assassinations of female activists, Communist cadres, and their supporters, was a failure, at least in the short run, as women who had given up the veil returned to the ancient practice. "For the most part, women may be said to have failed to function as a social class, a stratum with a sense of shared identity, with a distinct, clearly perceived community of experience, interest, purpose, and action."[47]

The Bolsheviks had little effective control over the countryside in their first decade in power, either in Russia or among the non-Russians of the periphery. Immediately after the October Revolution and until the civil war, Lenin's reach beyond Moscow, Petrograd, and a few loyal cities like Bolshevik-dominated Baku was quite weak, and for the first half-year of Soviet power, peasants and provincials largely ran their own affairs.[48] This began to change as the battle lines formed, and each side forcefully established its hold on local governmental bodies. Not only did military operations stem from political decisions, but politics was an extension of military moves. With the defeat of the anti-Bolsheviks, the Communists established their hold over towns and cities but were too few to control the countryside firmly. In the ethnic peripheries, those among the local elites who had survived the war reasserted their traditional roles. Among the Kazakhs, for example, soviet power was a facade that disguised the real structure of local power underneath.

The local power structure was controlled by the traditional clanic leaders. Aul [migratory unit, or settlement] soviets were formed in every community, as legislation required, but they were dominated by traditional leadership, both clanic and clerical. The same was true of the aul party cells; many communities had neither a party cell nor any aul Communists. However, where cells did exist the membership was indistinguishable from the traditional leadership groups. Both the general members and the local party secretaries had no secular education and knew nothing about either party ideology or party programs.[49]

The local, traditional sociocultural systems of the prerevolutionary period, segmented and small in scale, were resistant to forced change and provided havens from Soviet interventions. A Western anthropologist doing her field work in Georgia, for example, observed that "the sense of powerlessness of villagers towards the state encourages them to turn inwards."[50] Kinship networks and the mistrust of outsiders encouraged the use of unofficial, informal means of settling conflicts. Socialization still takes place in the family, and women as the guardians of the Georgian tradition have taught their children both the values of the culture and a wariness toward the larger Soviet world.[51] Patronage networks, so central in Transcaucasia to an individual's power and prestige, were carefully maintained and adapted to the requirements of an economy of shortages.[52]

Older ways of living, traditional networks, and established values were sources of strength to non-Russians that empowered them to resist outside impositions or adapt alien institutions to their own purposes. Collective farms in Tajikistan were based on the traditional kinship networks, the *avlod*, and were seen as belonging to the kinship group. Work brigades were made up of relatives.[53] Even industrial workers maintained traditional ways—marrying young, leaving seasonally for the village to cultivate the family plot, resisting emigration outside Central Asia. The government constantly but futilely fought against elaborate Georgian funerals, extended North Caucasian weddings and festivals, and those rites and rituals which it considered "remnants" of the feudal past. Without underestimating the degree to which life, even in the most isolated mountain villages, was shaped by the intervention of the Soviet state, the persistence of older customs and practices is impressive. And perhaps most frustrating for the central government was the close connection between kinship, culture, and the "second economy," the illegal wheeling and dealing protected by favors and bribes, family loyalties, and codes of silence.[54]

In her ethnography of a Georgian village, Tamara Dragadze demonstrates that even collectivization did little to change traditional settlement patterns or redistribute wealth in the villages of Ratcha. Family solidarity was actually fostered rather than undercut by Soviet practices.

> Soviet law re-enforces the age-old tradition whereby a son lives next to his parents, with nearby houses belonging to his brothers, paternal uncles and first cousins. . . . Throughout the country, the family provides more support and demands greater loyalty than any other institution. The government has refrained from interfering in this, except for campaigning against nepotism and overspending at family celebrations.[55]

The very nature of Soviet economic development created sharp divisions not only between but also within nationalities, between the more traditional and the radically transformed. Soviet economic and social change was extremely uneven, resulting in the coexistence of mobile, better-educated, more "modern" urban populations and less mobile, less well-educated, "traditional" societies in the countryside. In part this was due to a lack of resources, which made the full transformation of all parts of Soviet society economically too costly; but Soviet policies also contributed to the situation, whether consciously or unconsciously. Facing a choice between large-scale economic change and a cultural revolution, the Stalinist regime retreated from the more radical cultural practices of the 1920s and tolerated "distinctly uneven development in political, economic, and socio-cultural spheres—indeed [displayed] a willingness to leave pockets of antecedent life-styles relatively undisturbed, if necessary, for an indefinite period of time."[56]

Localism

The political leadership of the Communist party, even as it proclaimed the full resolution of the "national question" in the Soviet Union, failed to deal effectively with the problems of a multinational empire and allowed old tensions to fester. Bolshevism had long reduced problems of nationality and ethnic culture to economics, failing to appreciate the independent power of ethnic culture. Though it granted that nationality had to be accommodated before communism could claim a full victory, Bolshevism was consistently suspicious of national expression. Bolshevik policy was profoundly inconsistent, pushing for "nativization" and the "flourishing" (*rastsvet*) of national cultures while promoting the ideological goals of *stiranie* (obliteration of national peculiarities), *sblizhenie* (rapprochement), and *sliianie* (merging). The regime retained full power to decide what was permissible "patriotic" expression and what was pernicious nationalism, and the boundary between the two shifted constantly.[57]

When the center's control loosened after Stalin's death, regional and ethnic communist parties were permitted a considerable degree of independence from Moscow. In the Khrushchev and Brezhnev years, the arena of allowable national expression expanded significantly as republican leaderships forged their own ties with their populations through the manipulation of ethnic symbols. Though ultimate power and effective sovereignty remained with the central party authorities in Moscow until the early 1990s, in many republics local party elites were able to circumvent the center's control as long as economic growth continued and the worst excesses of nationalism were contained.

Once Stalinist terror was reduced—and in the absence of effective democratic control from below—the republics were essentially ruled by national "mafias," centered within the Communist parties and state apparatuses, whose reach extended throughout society. With the establishment of "indirect rule" from the center under Khrushchev and the easing of the extraordinary restrictions on ethnic expression, the national political elites, particularly in Transcaucasia and Central Asia, promoted a corrupt system of patronage, favoritism toward the titular nationality, and the widespread practice of bribe-taking and payoffs.[58] With the rise of complex networks of patrons and clients and "family circles," party leaders, like Vasilii Mzhavanadze in Georgia, Anton Kochinian in Armenia, and Veli Akhundov in Azerbaijan, men who had enjoyed Khrushchev's favor, became enmeshed in the corruption and favoritism that characterized normal Transcaucasian political and economic practices. Their tenures were marked by extraordinary longevity. Mzhavanadze was first secretary of the Georgian Communist party for nineteen years (1953–72). Kochinian had served as chairman of the Council of Ministers of Armenia (1952–66) before being tapped by Brezhnev to be Armenian first secretary (1966–74). Akhundov had succeeded Imam Mustafaev (1954–59), who had been ousted for corruption and national "isolationism," and spent ten years as first secretary of the Azerbaijani party.

The same trend toward long tenure was evident throughout the Soviet Union. In Uzbekistan, Sharaf Rashidov, a man whose name has become synonymous with corruption, ruled from 1959 until his death in 1983; in Tajikistan, Jabar Rasulov was party chief for 21 years (1961–82); in Kyrgyzstan, Turdakun Usubaliev ruled for 24 years (1961–85); Dinamukhammed Kunaev headed the Kazakh party for 22 years (1964–86); and Mukhamednazar Gapurov was Turkmen party chief for 16 years (1969–85). The situation was similar in the Soviet west: Pyotr Masherov ruled in Belorussia from 1965 to 1983; Ivan Bodyul in Moldavia from 1961 to 1980; I. G. Kebin in Estonia from 1950 to 1978; August Voss in Latvia from 1966 to 1984; and P. P. Grishkiavichius in Lithuania from 1974 to 1987. Ukraine, the largest non-Russian republic, saw its first Ukrainian first secretary, O. I. Kyrychenko (A. Kirichenko), appointed just after Stalin's death in 1953. But it was not until after his successor, M. Pidhornyi (N. Podgorny; 1957–63) was replaced by P. I. Shelest that Ukrainization of the party apparatus and the educational system accelerated. In 1972 Shelest was dismissed and Ukrainization was reined in under the loyal Brezhnevist V. V. Shcherbyts'ski, who ruled until just before his own death in 1989.[59] The longevity of these national leaderships had by the early 1970s led to the consolidation of local elites, who placated the local populations with moderate concessions to nationalist feelings and a high degree of economic permissiveness.

By the end of the 1960s, the Brezhnev regime, which in general backed the entrenched party cadres, found it difficult to tolerate the continued frustration of its economic plans. In order to break through the complex networks of friends, clients, and relatives erected by local party bosses in Transcaucasia, the central party leaders turned to new personnel outside the dominant party apparatuses. On July 14, 1969, Heidar Aliev, a career KGB officer, was selected as first secretary of the Azerbaijani Communist party. Three years later, in September 1972, his colleague in the Georgian security forces, Eduard Shevardnadze, was named leader of the Georgian party. That same year, Russians were brought into Armenia to serve as second secretary of the Central Committee and head of the KGB, and in November 1974, Karen Demirchian, a young Armenian engineer educated outside of Armenia, became party chief in Armenia.

The mandate given these men was the same: to end

economic and political corruption, to stimulate economic growth, to end ethnic favoritism and contain the more overt expressions of local nationalism, and to promote a new governing elite able to carry out the policies of the Communist party. But the underground economy and corrupt political practices in Transcaucasia and Central Asia proved to be particularly resistant to reform. Among the peoples of the Soviet south, loyalty is given first to kinship groups or intimate friends; a sense of personal worth therefore stems more from the honor or shame one brings on one's circle than from a successful career or great accumulation of wealth.[60] Favors done or received are the operative currency of both social and political relations. So powerful are the obligations to one's relatives and friends that the shame incurred by nonfulfillment was, for many in the southern tier of Soviet republics, much more serious than the penalties imposed by law. Indeed, since the political and police structures were also penetrated by such personal networks, protection from punishment was a frequent favor, and noncompliance with the law held fewer risks than did breaking family codes. Even after the state came down hard on the "second economy" in the 1970s and the risks involved in circumventing the law increased, the networks persisted, an effective form of national resistance to the ways of doing business imposed by the Soviet polity.

National Mobilization

Ironically, the Soviet state, which had been originally conceived as a state representing the historic role of a single class, the proletariat, had over time eroded the very sense of class that had brought the Bolsheviks to power. Through the 1920s and 1930s, the artificial manipulation of class categories and official restrictions on autonomous class activity undermined identification with and loyalty to class. The "dictatorship of the proletariat" was eventually replaced by a "state of the whole people." In 1974, the very designation of class, so key to identity, privilege, and advantage in the 1920s, was eliminated from Soviet passports.

Yet nationality had through the same decades taken on a new importance as an indicator of membership in a relevant social and cultural community. In the Union republics, membership in the titular nationality conferred various advantages, both through the official "affirmative-action" programs that promoted the local peoples and through informal networks based on kinship, religion, and language. With the emergence of an articulated civil society in the Soviet Union in the post-Stalin decades, identification with nationality was for most non-Russians a far more palpable touchstone than the eroded loyalty to social class.

The end of terror and the first serious questioning of the seamless Stalinist version of history in 1956 drove the regime to seek other forms of authority and legitimation. Despite the continued rhetorical commitment to internationalism, non-Russian leaderships attempted to ground their regimes in toothless national appeals. Republic leaders promoted their own local forms of "official nationalism," celebrations of sanctioned traditions and acceptable heroes of the past. Certain figures from the reconstructed histories of the Soviet nationalities were incorporated into the official narrative; others were excluded. In Georgia, for example, the leading nationalist poet of the nineteenth century, Ilia Chavchavadze, was sanctified as part of the canon, despite his hostility to socialism and his Armenophobic chauvinism, whereas the leader of the independent Menshevik republic, Noe Zhordania, himself a committed Marxist, was anathematized. The boundaries of official nationalism were heatedly negotiated between intellectuals and the state. Although "nationalist" expression was severely limited in Ukraine after the fall of Shelest, in Armenia monuments were erected to unorthodox revolutionary figures, like General Antranik, and religious heroes, like Saint Vartan.

Though "official nationalism," or what is defined by Soviet authorities as "patriotism," became a permissible form of expression in the more laissez-faire atmosphere of the 1950s and 1960s, central authorities, always wary of potential ethnic chauvinism or political separatism, periodically reined in the more vocal proponents of local nationalism. Beyond the frontier of the permitted expression of ethnic pride and historical achievement, there appeared in the 1960s a dissident or "unorthodox" nationalism expressed by a few human-rights activists and even revolutionary separatists. As early as March 1956, students in Tbilisi took to the streets in an essentially nationalist protest against the removal of a monument to Stalin and were met by gunfire from the army. Dozens were killed. Almost a decade later, on April 24, 1965, thousands of Armenians marched in an unofficial demonstration to mark the fiftieth anniversary of the Genocide. Then First Secretary Zakov Zarobian rejected the use of force and tried to calm the crowds. As a concession to Armenian national sentiments, a monument to the victims of the massacres and deportations of 1915 was built on a hill in Erevan, Tsitsernakaberd, and each year on April 24, spontaneous processions of people file up to the eternal flame to lay flowers. But Zarobian, who had achieved considerable popularity in Armenia for his conciliatory attitude toward Armenian national feelings, was removed from power within a year after the demonstration.

As state and society struggled over the definition of national rights in the Brezhnev years, the openly defiant dissident movement risked arrest and exile to express its political discontentedness. More a symptom of a deep malaise within Soviet society than an attempt to provide an effective alternative to the extant national leadership, the appearance of nationalist dissidents nevertheless was indicative of the erosion of faith in the "socialist choice," in which many party officials themselves no longer believed. The various oppositional and dissident movements, some based in campaigns for human rights, others more specifically nationalist or religious, found greater resonance in the Western press than in Soviet society at large. But those dissident movements firmly rooted in ethnic and linguistic issues found the greatest response in the population.[61]

The explosive power of national identification and the reluctance of the Soviet government to push too hard against it was demonstrated vividly in the April 1978 protest by hundreds of students and others in Tbilisi against a government plan to change the clause in the Georgian constitution that proclaimed Georgian to be the state language of the republic. With the coming to power of new national leaderships in 1969–74, renewed emphasis had been placed on the need for Russian-language education and the curbing of what Shevardnadze called "national narrow-mindedness and isolation." Now the Georgian party chief was forced to address an angry crowd, estimated at 5,000, before the building of the Council of Ministers, and to inform them that he had recommended recognition of Georgian as the state language.[62] Not only was Georgian retained, but similar proposed changes in the constitutions of Armenia and Azerbaijan were prudently abandoned. No party leaders suffered from this open expression of anti-Russian sentiment, which may be seen as an early manifestation of the re-emergence of civil society in the Soviet Union and a harbinger of *perestroika* from below.

The dissident nationalist movements were divided between a small number of revolutionary separatists, like the Armenian National Unity Party, and more moderate intellectuals who formed human-rights organizations, like the short-lived Helsinki Watch Committees that attempted to awaken international public opinion to the denial of national rights within the Soviet Union.[63] Dissidents in Georgia, for example, at first became interested in the seemingly anodyne pursuit of preservation of Georgia's historic and religious monuments, but some of the most daring soon took up the plight of the Meskhetians, Muslim Georgians who had been forcibly moved in 1944 from their homes along the Turkish border to Central Asia and wanted to return. Many of these dissidents were arrested, and by the early 1980s they had either disappeared underground or been exiled abroad. Out of the "unorthodox" nationalist movements of the Brezhnev years came many of the activists who later would lead the mass nationalisms of the Gorbachev period.[64]

Nations Within the Empire

On the rare occasions when Sovietological literature focused on the non-Russian peoples, the argument was made that the Soviet state had effectively subdued and integrated the nationalities into the general project of social transformation. As long as the dominant interpretative model was almost entirely state-centered, analysts agreed that the result of the totalitarian assault on the peripheries, as on society in general, was to atomize subjects and render resistance impossible. Even when Western social science revisioned Soviet industrialization as one alternative form of modernization, the expectation remained that non-Russians would succumb to the social rewards and material benefits of assimilation into Soviet culture. Only in the 1970s did a few students of the "national question" begin to emphasize the deeply contradictory policies and processes that were creating new capacities for resistance to the creation of a single *sovetskii narod* (Soviet people).

Leninist nationality policy established a particular framework—state structures based on ethnicity, policies of nativization, a pseudofederal polity—in which the future history of non-Russians would be shaped. Though Moscow's imperial reach often ignored the prerogatives of the republics, rendering their sovereignty a fiction, many nationalities became demographically more consolidated within their "homelands," acquired effective and articulate national political and intellectual elites, and developed a shared national consciousness. These more conscious and consolidated nationalities were "rooted" to specific territories, with abundant privileges for the titular nations and their local Communist elites. The economic and social transformation associated with the brutalities of Stalinism undermined but never eliminated the cultural and social gains of non-Russians. Indeed, many older forms of association were preserved, despite the catastrophes of collectivization and the Great Purges.

With the end of Terror and the reduction of the hypercentralism of the Stalin years, local elites made a greater effort to rule through persuasion, concessions, and "delivering the goods" to their own constituents. Greater permissiveness for nationalist expression went along in many republics with the elaboration of mafia-like networks of kinfolk and clans that linked local political power with expansion of the "second economy." The growing corruption in the republics was sanctioned in the late Brezhnev period by the very top of the party, and the degeneration of the system was well advanced by the time a new generation of leaders attempted to stem the decay.

Those policies and processes that strengthened the nationalities in their own republic deeply conflicted with contradictory policies and processes that pulled non-Russians toward acculturation, even assimilation, into a general, Russified Soviet culture. In the western Soviet republics, Russification took a toll in the Stalin and post-Stalin periods. Many non-Russians, especially intellectuals, became anxious about the ever-present threat to the national from the stated policies and practices of the Soviet regime. In the last several decades of the Soviet state, growing disillusionment in society with the goals and the competence of Soviet leaders was increasingly expressed, quietly, in the idiom of nationalism. By its own usurpation of the language of class, the Soviet state had delegitimized it as a rhetoric of dissent and, ironically, authorized ethnicity as an alternative mode of oppositional expression.

One can argue that nationalism has been a growing presence in all parts of the world in our century, that the very processes of urbanization and industrialization, the spread of mass education and greater access to print and other media, aid the consolidation of ethnolinguistic groups—all within a powerful, universal discourse of the nation. But nation-making in the USSR occurred within a unique context: a state that had set out to overcome nationalism and the differences between nations had in fact created a set of institutions and initiated processes that fostered the development of conscious, secular, politically mobilizable nationalities. Despite the stated goals of the Communist party, the processes of nativization, industrialization, urbanization, and state-building in the Soviet Union provided the social and cultural base, first, for ethnic elites to organize low-level resistance to rule by Russia and, later, for counterelites to mobilize broad-based nationalist movements. Still, the open challenge to the empire came only after the top party leadership decided to reform radically the political system, only when Communists themselves began a process that delegitimized the Soviet system and allowed a political voice to the nationalist alternative.

CHAPTER 4

Nationalism and Nation-States: Gorbachev's Dilemmas

When Gorbachev came to power in March 1985, the Soviet state was already in a profoundly weakened condition. The USSR had experienced not only years of political and economic stagnation but also a frustrating absence of able and stable leadership in the first half of the 1980s. Weakness in the center had enabled the local ethnic and regional mafias within the party-state apparatus to increase their power. Moreover, the USSR was internationally isolated, bogged down in a draining war in Afghanistan, and facing an aggressively hostile American president. In order to restart the Soviet economic engine and restore the country's position internationally, Gorbachev needed first to build a political base for his program of reform, not least in the non-Russian republics. "Probably the most concentrated opposition to Gorbachev's leadership and his policies," writes Martha Brill Olcott, "has come from the party and state bureaucracies in the national republics."[1]

Gorbachev was caught between nationality leaderships that opposed his reforms, and intellectual and popular forces, most of which, once they overcame their suspicion of the Kremlin, were interested in the general liberalizing thrust of Moscow's new policies. In nearly every Transcaucasian and Central Asian republic, a series of purges (1985–88) eliminated the top leaders, though not always without resistance. In Kazakhstan, the removal of long-time party chief Dinmukhammed Kunaev and his replacement by a Russian, Gennadii Kolbin, brought demonstrators into the streets in December 1986. Prolonged pressure from the center on the Armenian party did not achieve the desired removal of Karen Demirchian from the post of first secretary until the Karabagh crisis exploded and Moscow could more directly intervene. But the political control over the republics by local mafias or party machines was hardly touched by these interventions.

When the "democratic" forces began to act, as with the Karabagh movement, the emergence of mass nationalist popular fronts burst the very bounds of the old politics in a number of republics—Armenia, Georgia, the Baltic republics—and rapidly undermined the power of local Communist parties, even those whose leaderships had been renewed. In other republics, however—in Central Asia most particularly—*perestroika* from below was contained and Communist *apparatchiki* maintained their hold on both state and society. With the general democratization of political practices, the delegitimization of Communist party rule in the center, and the growing reluctance and inability of Moscow to use force to impose its will (what was called, after April 9, 1989, the "Tbilisi syndrome"), the old political classes were either pushed from power by nationalist movements or had to cover themselves with the mantle of nationalism.

The Odd Empire

Despite the reluctance of many scholars and publicists to call the Soviet Union an empire, that conventional description revealed certain buried truths about the nature of the federation. If one thinks of an empire as a state or system of states made up of diverse peoples in which one group is privileged in its relationship with the central authority and other subordinate peoples, the Soviet Union appears to fit the bill. An inequitable relationship existed between the ruling elite and the great mass of the population, and membership in that elite was predicated on a successful adaptation to "Soviet" norms of behavior that involved Russian language and cultural skills. Russians and Slavs were overrepresented in institutions of power; non-Russians identified the power elites as "Russian"; and the whole hierarchical arrangement of subordination and superordination was masked by the rhetoric of internationalism. The original impulses of Lenin's nationality policies, intended to reverse Russian privilege and undermine Great Power Chauvinism, had long ago been distorted by the dominance of a single Communist party that stripped the federal units of any meaningful political autonomy and by the Stalinist policies that disallowed "national communisms" in the border republics. At the same time, many ethnic Russians felt burdened by the "costs" of empire and "exploited" by the peripheries. At least a semblance of nationhood had been permitted the major non-Russian peoples, whereas Great Russians were much more limited in manifesting their ethnic national aspirations or enjoying the institutions and privileges of a nation-state. Buried within a federation within a federation, the Russian "nation" experienced the same sense of peril that smaller peoples of the Soviet Union felt. The nation was in danger, its heritage squandered, its monuments crumbling, the memory of its past distorted almost beyond recovery. By the late 1980s, the Soviet system was not working even for its dominant nationality.

Moscow had governed through local national cadres and promoted national cultures, education in the local languages, and the advancement of native leaders—all within the bounds of a policy that favored the eventual creation of a single *sovetskii narod* (Soviet people). The Soviet state's deeply contradictory policy nourished the cultural uniqueness of distinct peoples. It thereby increased ethnic solidarity and national consciousness in the non-Russian republics, even as it frustrated full articulation of a national agenda by requiring conformity to an imposed political order. In important ways, the Soviet empire was like other empires that "modernized" through economic development programs but facilitated the possibility of communication and interaction, repression and reproduction of cultural practices, making nationality more articulate and nationalism the most potent expression of denied ambitions.

Between center and periphery, power relations were always unequal and limiting, but in the 74 years of Soviet power, the subject nationalities gained their own subsidized intelligentsias, institutionalized in republican universities and academies of sciences, as well as a new demographic presence in their own capital cities. The tensions between the emerging nations fostered by Soviet policies and the maintenance of empire became ever more difficult to contain within acceptable bounds.[2] Under Khrushchev and Brezhnev, much authority was surrendered to the local national elites that ran the republics, particularly in Central Asia and Transcaucasia, as fiefdoms to be exploited for the benefit of the local party aristocracy. Corruption and nationalism grew hand in hand, limiting the Kremlin's writ in the borderlands. Not surprisingly, the high living of many Caucasians and Central Asians confirmed for Russians their belief that the mode of exploitation in the USSR ran from center to periphery, rather than from colony to metropole as in more traditional empires. In fact, the non-Russian republics, particularly those of the south, benefited from cheap Russian resources, investment, and factory production, as well as from Russians who migrated as laborers to their regions.

The Soviet empire in the post-Stalin decades maintained itself through tolerance of diversity and local national control with the ultimate sanction of the threat or use of armed force (as in Tbilisi in 1956, Erevan in 1965, Alma-Ata in 1986, and Baku in 1990). But underneath the deceptive stability of the political structures, a fuse had already been lit by the 1960s—with the appearance of a powerful, articulate civil society expressing itself in a national idiom. Though effectively contained until the Gorbachev revolution, the dissident movements of the 1960s through the 1980s shaped the oppositional discourse and generated the leaders (Levon Ter Petrosyan in Armenia, Zviad Gamsakhurdia in Georgia, Ivan Drach in Ukraine, to mention but a few) who would emerge as spokespeople for the nation in the late 1980s. Nation and democracy both proved to be subversive to empire, for neither would tolerate the supranational relationship of superordination and subordination dictated by the imperial system.

Gorbachev and the Road to a New State Structure

In the already enormous and still-growing literature on the Gorbachev revolution, at least three general views on the prospects of reform in the USSR have emerged. The most prominent in the West for much of the first five years of Gorbachev's rule was a conservative, mostly pessimistic view that real reform toward a modern democratic state was impossible within the USSR, that either the efforts of the general secretary were insincere or the built-in resistance of Russia's political culture or the Soviet bureaucracy doomed to failure his plans for reform.[3] Here Gorbachev, like his mentor Andropov, was seen as a kind of dynamic Brezhnev, whose limited reforms were meant to integrate Western technology and productivity into an essentially post-Stalinist

2

party-state. The Brezhnev record, however, had shown that although such limited Western borrowings might have created a militarily powerful adversary, they could not reverse the economic stagnation.

Less often present in the Sovietological discourse but available in the media was a liberal and optimistic view that Gorbachev intended (and would be able to carry out) a radical, indeed revolutionizing reform that would bring the Soviet Union back to the tolerant pluralism of the New Economic Policy and possibly further into a democratic polity and market socialism.[4] A third view, muted at first but increasingly vocal after the 1989 revolutions in East Central Europe, held that Gorbachev's reform from above would necessarily have to be radicalized, would move to marketization, and would likely lead to the collapse of the Soviet Union as we have known it.[5]

All three views recognized that radicalization of the reforms presented enormous dangers, but none foresaw the way in which the revolution from above would be hijacked by nationalist revolutions from below that could not be contained within Gorbachev's limited vision. The development of civil society and coherent, conscious nations within the USSR inexorably transformed Gorbachev's efforts at state-building into a liberating process of state-dismantling. The first mass resistance that could not be contained within the metamorphosing Soviet system, the crisis that precipitated the unraveling of central Soviet authority, came from an Armenian enclave in the republic of Azerbaijan.

Crisis over Karabagh

An autonomous region now entirely within Azerbaijan, Nagorno- or "Mountainous" Karabagh had through the centuries been a marchland between the Muslims of the plains and the Christians of the mountains. Semi-independent Armenian princes had governed Karabagh (Artsakh to the Armenians) in early modern times, but when Transcaucasia was annexed by the Russian empire, Karabagh was linked administratively with the richer agricultural plains to the east. After the revolution, the Bolsheviks promised Karabagh to Armenia, but once again pragmatism won out. Given the poverty of Armenia, the relative wealth of oil-rich Azerbaijan, and Soviet reluctance to offend their ally Mustapha Kemal, the Nagorno-Karabagh Autonomous District (NKAO) was established within Azerbaijan. At the same time another region, Nakhichevan, which contained a large Armenian minority and was physically separated from the rest of Azerbaijan by Armenian territory, was declared an autonomous republic (a higher designation), also under the jurisdiction of Azerbaijan.

By 1979 the proportion of Armenians in Karabagh had fallen from about 85 percent to 75 percent of the population. Local Armenians, supported by their compatriots in the Armenian republic, claimed that the region was being kept backward by the Azerbaijani government and that Armenians were being encouraged to emigrate. Fearing a fate similar to that of Nakhichevan, where the Armenian population had fallen from nearly half to less than 10 percent of the total population in the Soviet period, Armenian activists in both Karabagh and Armenia proper began to agitate for the incorporation of Karabagh into Armenia in the 1960s. The central Soviet government repeatedly affirmed that Karabagh would remain part of Azerbaijan. Suddenly, unpredictably, on February 13, 1988, the Karabagh Armenians, inspired by the rhetoric of *perestroika* and encouraged by regime attacks on old-style party rule, began a series of demonstrations in favor of union with Armenia. Five days later, Gorbachev tried to placate them by offering to hold a special session of the Central Committee to discuss state policy toward the nationalities. The very next day, thousands marched in

Erevan in support of Karabagh, and an unprecedented ethnopolitical crisis faced the Kremlin. In a historic move, the
Karabagh soviet, usually nothing more than a transmitter of
party policy, voted 110 to 17 to intercede with the Supreme
Soviet of the USSR for the transfer of Karabagh to Armenia.

When authorities in Moscow hesitated and appeared to be
confused, the movement grew, until by the last week of February hundreds of thousands were marching in Erevan in
continuous demonstrations. Azerbaijanis, reacting to the
Armenian demands, took to the streets. For two days, February 28–29, rioters roamed the Azerbaijani industrial town of
Sumgait in search of Armenian victims. Busses were stopped
and searched, hospitals and apartments invaded. Before military forces could quell the riots, 31 people were dead and
hundreds injured.

Azerbaijani intellectuals and officials condemned the riots
but maintained that Karabagh was historically a part of their
homeland. The Gorbachev government faced a serious crisis
for which neither the Soviet Constitution nor political pre-
cedent provided much guidance—the need to settle a violently contested territorial conflict between two union republics. Each nationality set out exclusive historic claims to
the region. Armenians, who constituted the demographic
majority, bolstered their claim with arguments based on
democratic principles and even Leninist notions of self-
determination. Azerbaijanis countered with defenses of territorial integrity and constitutionalism.

With Sumgait, the possibility of a peaceful transfer of Karabagh to Armenia became remote. As attitudes on both
sides hardened, a mediated settlement satisfactory to both
parties became extremely unlikely. Karabagh was placed under direct rule from Moscow for a year and a half (July 1988
to November 1989), but the fighting only intensified. A powerful national front formed in Armenia (the Karabagh Committee, later the Armenian National Movement [*Haiots*

Hamazgain Sharzhum or HHSh]). Its leaders came from the professional intelligentsia, most of them opposed to the corrupt Communist leadership in the republic. They combined Armenian nationalism with ecological concerns and a firm commitment to democratic politics.

In Azerbaijan, similarly placed intellectuals created the Azerbaijan People's Front (*Azarbayjan Khalg Jabhasi* or AKhJ), though they never acquired the degree of authority, organization, and discipline over the crowds that the Armenian nationalists achieved. AKhJ represented a momentary ascendency of the power and influence of part of the national intelligentsia that was soon lost when less-educated and less-privileged people began mobilizing. In mid-November 1988, mass rallies in Baku protested what they held to be Armenian encroachments on Azerbaijani authority in Karabagh. Led by a dynamic young worker, Neimat Panakhov, speakers denounced the Communist leadership and the urban intelligentsia. The AKhJ was torn socially and politically between those concerned with the many problems facing Azerbaijani society and those who wanted to concentrate on the Karabagh question. The pull toward democratizing Azerbaijani society faltered on the Karabagh issue, because no important Azerbaijani intellectual or politician would agree to self-determination in Karabagh.

The complete breakdown of the interethnic symbiosis in Azerbaijan and Armenia, compounded by the simultaneous demands for greater autonomy in the Baltic region, led Gorbachev to warn the non-Russians that the future of *perestroika* was at stake. "We are one family," he pleaded; "we have one common home."[6] But anger and fear in both Armenia and Azerbaijan could not be overcome with pleas or postponements, and Gorbachev's hesitant and inconsistent policies toward the non-Russian nationalities eroded the sympathy and support he had initially enjoyed.

Tens of thousands of Armenian refugees began leaving

Azerbaijan for Armenia, and by late 1988 hundreds of thousands of Azerbaijanis, fearing reprisals, migrated from Armenia. The Azerbaijani refugees, largely migrants from rural Armenia, ended up in Baku and other cities in an inhospitable environment troubled by high unemployment. They were outsiders in their own homeland, resentful of the Armenians who had pressured them to leave their villages. These unsettled migrants, it was later reported, made up the bulk of the crowds that savaged the Armenians in Baku in January 1990.

Many of the now-homeless Armenians from Azerbaijan settled in Leninakan and Kirovakan, just days before a massive earthquake devastated these second- and third-largest cities of the republic. As 1988 came to an end, Armenians, stunned by the double tragedy imposed by nature and by their neighbors, tried to sort out the dismal results of a year of political promises and frustrated hopes. Gorbachev, who had seen his triumphal visit to the United States cut short by the devastation in Armenia, ordered the arrest of the leaders of the Karabagh Committee and the Azerbaijani movement. For the next six months, Moscow attempted to shore up Communist party authority in Armenia and Azerbaijan, to rule those republics in the old way, without the participation of an awakened society. By late spring that approach had to be abandoned. Once released, the leaders of the Karabagh movement began their long trek toward dismantling communism and creating an Armenian democracy.

By the end of 1989, the nationalist movements had all but displaced the official power structure in the Transcaucasian republics. In Azerbaijan, the People's Front, increasingly hostile to the Communist party, effectively organized a blockade against the Armenia republic in August and initiated strikes and demonstrations to force the Azerbaijani Supreme Soviet to declare Azerbaijan a "sovereign socialist state" within the USSR. By November, the Communist party of

Azerbaijan had essentially capitulated to the Front, and in order to stop the blockade and demonstrations Moscow ended its direct rule over Karabagh and restored the authority of the local soviet (November 28). In other parts of the republic, local militants challenged the discredited Communist apparatus. In Lenkoran, the nationalists effectively controlled the towns. In December, the protestors in Nakhichevan tore down border markers and guard posts along the Soviet-Iranian border to "reunite" "Southern Azerbaijan" and the Soviet republic, something long desired by Soviet Azerbaijani intellectuals.[7]

Mass rallies called for the separation of Azerbaijan from the USSR, and in January 1990, groups of extremists broke from a large rally and began massacring Armenians in Baku. After a year and a half of trying to avoid direct military intervention, Gorbachev declared a state of emergency in Azerbaijan and dispatched troops, first to Karabagh and then to Baku. Most of the Armenians in the city had been either killed or evacuated by the time the army entered the city. Hundreds of Azerbaijanis were killed as armored columns brutally crushed manned barricades; dozens were arrested as the Soviet army, in a desperate campaign, attempted to restore authority to the discredited Azerbaijani Communist party.

Forced to face the most fundamental of Soviet dilemmas—how to democratize and modernize the largest country on the globe while maintaining the last multinational empire—Gorbachev finally, reluctantly, exercised the full armed power of the state. Unlike the national struggles in the Soviet Baltic, which were largely free of popular violence, the Armenian-Azerbaijani conflict over the Karabagh was far more volatile, less manipulable by political authorities, and more subject to rapid and unpredictable escalation. It could be resolved by neither persuasion nor repression, and in the very determination and intransigence of its par- *O* ticipants, the Karabagh conflict revealed the inadequacies of the Soviet constitutional order and the growing weakness of cohesive elements within the federation other than armed force.

From Reform to Revolution

Mindful of the failures of the last major efforts at reform by Khrushchev and Kosygin, Gorbachev and his small group of reform-minded politicians understood that success depended on the implementation of a strategy that would accomplish three goals simultaneously: democratization (or at least neutralization) of the conservative *apparat*; mobilization of civil society, particularly the "liberal" intelligentsia, both to criticize the old system and its practitioners and to stimulate popular participation in *perestroika*; and initiation of a series of political and economic reforms that would both erode the power of the conservatives, centered in the Communist party apparatus, and institutionalize democracy within both society and the party. This strategy was fraught with dangers and required maneuvering between the conservatives and the liberals, placating one without frightening the other, all the time pulling the country toward democratic reform.

Gorbachev skillfully held together a broad coalition of party leaders, from Aleksandr Yakovlev and Boris Yeltsin on his left to Yegor Ligachev on his right, and gradually undermined the centers of Communist power. But his necessary vacillations—first to the side of reform, then toward retrenchment—his inability to control extramural disruptions and violence, and the worsening economic crisis combined to undermine his popularity and authority and to polarize Left and Right.[8] Brezhnev's strategy had been to prevent any significant reform at home while maintaining the empire abroad and borrowing from the West. Gorbachev reversed this strategy, linking domestic economic modernization to a retreatist policy abroad—the withdrawal from Afghanistan and East Central Europe, major concessions on arms reductions, collaboration with American leadership in the Gulf War—in the hope that conversion of military spending would prime the economic pump at home and that aid would be forthcoming from less-threatened capitalist countries.

What Gorbachev himself did not fully realize was the extent to which the USSR was no longer (if it had ever been, except under the forced homogenization of Stalinism) a single society. The fiction of a united *sovetskii narod*, proposed and defended by Soviet theorists of ethnicity, certainly reflected important shared characteristics of many educated urban Soviet citizens, but it was belied by the powerful identification with nationality not only of those villagers untransformed by the Soviet experience, but also of many intellectuals. As we have seen, within the pseudofederalism of the Stalinist and post-Stalinist states, nations had grown up that were linked to specific territories formally established and bounded just before or during the Soviet period. In some cases, the titular nationality in a republic made up only a minority of the population, as in Kazakhstan, Tatarstan, or Abkhazia. Yet these nationalities were given cultural and political privileges within their ethnic territories; local elites were in control of political patronage; and their intelligentsia had a stake in the maintenance of strong, separate, territorially rooted nationalities. At the same time, as the Soviet economy ground down after the mid-1970s, one nationality after another began to express a profound anxiety about the threat to their culture, language, demographic, economic, and ecological future. In the USSR, the Green concern about the environment found its most consistent allies among the tricolor supporters of the national cause. In the emerging reconstruction of their own history, the nationalists identified the Soviet experiment as the enemy of essential, authentic, natural national aspirations. No concession to the formative influence of the Soviet experience in the making of nations entered the new discourse of separatism.

Breathing life into the moribund system that had uninhibitedly called itself socialist for so many decades required much more radical reconstruction than most Communists, even the general secretary himself, had foreseen. Gorbachev's first campaigns were modest indeed—the struggle against the plague of alcoholism and a campaign à la Andropov for greater labor discipline and productivity. Step by step, as if responding to an internal logic of reform, the progressives in the party improvised the dismantling of the "administrative-command system," but did not replace it with a working economy or an effective democratic polity. To demonstrate how systemic the stagnation that afflicted the country was, and to gain allies within the intelligentsia, Gorbachev promoted ever more open discussion of the ills of Soviet society. Faith in the socialist project had long since eroded among educated people, but the subversive power of the new criticism undermined what was left of the authority and influence of the party apparatus. *Glasnost'* eliminated within a few years the privileged position of Marxism-Leninism, and the rewriting of Soviet history moved back in time beyond the permitted critique of Stalinism into a fundamental rereading of Lenin's revolution. The nomenklatura's will to resist the popular discontent, now legitimized by the policy of *glasnost'*, dissipated. Spasmodic attempts by conservatives to reverse the trends set in motion by Gorbachev, such as the infamous Nina Andreeva letter of March 1988, only exposed their opposition to *perestroika*, which had become official party policy.

Gorbachev's reforms, so tentatively begun in the Andropov mode in 1985, rapidly evolved into a revolution after the Karabagh events of February 1988. After failing to win agreement from his own ruling party to democratize the apparatus from within through multicandidate elections, the general secretary proposed such elections to a new Congress of People's Deputies at the Nineteenth Party Conference in June 1988. These national, and later local, elections spelled the death of the Communist party's monopoly on political power. The outburst of mass nationalist movements, first in Transcaucasia and soon after in the Baltic republics, occurred at the same time. In Armenia, Georgia, Lithuania, Latvia, Estonia, Moldavia, and later Ukraine and Belorussia, intellectuals and activists began, first in the spirit of *glasnost'* and *perestroika* and carrying portraits of Gorbachev, to form national and popular fronts and to put forward ethnocultural demands against the Russifying programs of the Soviet Communist party. In Central Asia, on the other hand, where dissident movements had not previously existed and a closer relation between the apparatus and the intelligentsia was the norm, the Communist parties maintained their influence and managed to suppress the relatively weak "democratic" oppositions.

By the fall of 1988, both Estonians and Lithuanians had founded mass popular fronts. The Lithuanians successfully agitated to be allowed to display their national flag, and on November 16, Estonia declared itself a sovereign republic. Much of the struggle through 1988–89 focused on securing official recognition of the local language as the state language of the republic. When in April 1989 Soviet troops brutally crushed a huge demonstration in Tbilisi calling for Georgian independence, the reaction among the democratic forces, both in the relatively liberated press and in the opening sessions of the new Congress of People's Deputies, made it nearly impossible for the Kremlin to use armed force again against the burgeoning national movements. Gorbachev's more conservative comrades, led by Yegor Ligachev, who was implicated in the Georgian tragedy, were reined in for a time, and for the next year the Soviet army was used only where interethnic fighting necessitated armed mediation (Ferghana in June 1989, Azerbaijan in January 1990, Dushanbe in February 1990, Osh in June 1990).

By the end of 1990, all the union republics and most of the autonomous republics responded to the rapidly weakening central state and to the examples set by the former Eastern European satellites, declaring themselves sovereign, in several cases independent, states. The empire was dying, and the Gorbachev leadership accepted the fact that the new form of union/disunion was to be negotiated on the basis of equity and mutual respect. Gorbachev's commitment to democratic reform restrained the kind of physical force that had forged the empire and preserved it for seven decades.

Even as he chipped away at the party's power, Gorbachev remained the principal buffer between the Soviet Communist party and the fate of its brother parties in East Central Europe. His conservative opponents knew that if he were removed from his post by the *apparat*, the party would lose its last shred of legitimacy and support among the population. For those who feared that Gorbachev had created the conditions for the breakup of the Soviet Union, his political demise would realize just those anxieties. The separatist movements in the Baltic and the Caucasus would realize their programs of independence, and other republics would soon be encouraged to follow. At the same time, Gorbachev was eroding party authority, which was his own most effective instrument of power. The new state structures he created gave him prestige and international recognition, but as one who was reluctant to face a popular election, his ultimate legitimacy could be questioned.

No alternative to Gorbachev's increasingly radical reforms was articulated by influential political figures until the summer of 1990. From the Left he heard constant carping by radical intellectuals and politicians to go faster, but

Gorbachev believed that the Moscow and Leningrad demo-crats did not appreciate how isolated they were, how conservative much of the countryside remained, and how dangerous still were the "forces of order" in the KGB, MVD, and the army. Boris Yeltsin's populist opposition to the privileges of party position was attractive to voters, but his often brusque political style frightened moderate reformers, who stuck with the coalition-builder and pragmatic compromiser, Gorbachev. More ominous through 1990 were the subdued voices from the Right, like those of the leaders of the Russian Republic's Communist party and the Russian Writers' Union, that called for a return to discipline and order and flavored their appeals with chauvinism and anti-Semitism. With fewer goods to buy and the disruptions brought by new freedoms, a significant number of Soviet citizens responded to appeals for stability and grew nostalgic for the days when security and predictability had provided what comforts they had.

Gorbachev's preferred solution for the "national question" was a return to Lenin's nationality policy, a genuine federalism to replace the Stalinist emasculation of the federation. He spoke of restoring the violated rights of Soviet Germans, Crimean Tatars, Meskhetian Turks, Kalmyks, Balkars, Karachai, Chechens, Ingush, Greeks, Koreans, and Kurds, but he consistently rejected demands for redrawing the administrative boundaries in the USSR. "*Perestroika* is not *perekroika* [resewing]," he is purported to have said. But Lenin's policies toward the non-Russians had been, like so many of his other initiatives, a combination of principle and pragmatism. Gorbachev repeatedly opted for more pragmatic solutions to the interethnic conflicts that threatened his programs, but was confronted by the radical implications of Lenin's principles. National self-determination to the point of separation had been enshrined in a constitutional guarantee of a right of secession from the union, a time bomb that lay dormant through the years of Stalinism, only to explode with the Gorbachev reforms.

The end of the Communist monopolies on power in Eastern Europe and the abrupt end to the Cold War accelerated the drive for full independence by a number of nationalities. Whereas 1988–89 had been marked by a few declarations of sovereignty and the establishment of official languages in the republics, 1990 witnessed a succession of declarations of both sovereignty and independence, beginning with Lithuania's declaration of independence in March. Most threatening to Gorbachev was the election of Yeltsin as chair of the RSFSR Supreme Soviet and the subsequent declaration of sovereignty by the Russian republic. Though he did not identify himself with the more chauvinistic and anti-Semitic Russian nationalists, most of whom were deeply antidemocratic and anti-Western in their outlook, Yeltsin skillfully built a base of support for himself by combining populist opposition to Communist privileges, assertions of Russian nationhood, and an unwavering commitment to rapid democratization and marketization. Already prefigured in the growing rivalry between Gorbachev and Yeltsin were two models for the future of the Soviet Union—one that preserved the center and granted extensive though limited rights to the republics, and another that eroded the center into near nonexistence and dissolved the union into fifteen sovereign republics.

Despite his foreign-policy and domestic political successes, Gorbachev was plagued by his inability to effect economic reforms. Even after his election as president of the Soviet Union by the Congress of People's Deputies, his pressure on the Communist party to surrender its monopoly on power, and the implementation of a multiparty system early in 1990, drastic food shortages in Soviet cities eroded support both for Gorbachev personally and for his programs. His triple revolution—democratization, decolonization, marketization—

foundered on the third point. In the central cities, the major beneficiary was Yeltsin; in the republics, the winners were the nationalist leaderships, who, unlike Gorbachev, were willing to seek popular mandates in open, contested elections.

The Final Crisis

In the summer of 1990, the democratic opposition to Gorbachev acquired its own program of reform—the famous Shatalin Plan of radical economic reform within 500 days. Though more a sketch for change than a detailed plan, the 500-day program became the basis for a brief political alliance in late July between Gorbachev and Yeltsin. But while Shatalin was visiting the United States, Gorbachev retreated, perhaps fearful of the consequences both to the managerial elite and to the already burdened populace.[9] The Supreme Soviet approved a much more moderate plan for change, basically gutting the 500-day program and smashing the alliance with Yeltsin and the democratic reformers. Effective state power had been eroded by a "war of laws" between the central Soviet government and the republics, and presidential degrees could not be enforced locally. As Soviet political scientist Andranik Migranyan put it, "There is no verticality of power." The conservative turn was marked by efforts to shore up the eroding prestige and self-respect of the army. Gorbachev decreed that local officials could not refuse residence permits for out-of-republic servicemen who were performing their military service and that republics could not restrict the military draft and encourage draft evasion. Defense Minister General Yazov warned on television that all actions against the army would be punished. An *Izvestiia* correspondent noted that "a disrespected, defamed, and offended Army inevitably becomes socially dangerous."[10] As the crisis between the Baltic republics and the Kremlin heated up in November and the food crisis intensified on the eve of winter, Gorbachev hesitated to accelerate the reforms, and instead made a tactical accommodation with the conservative "forces of order."

Why Gorbachev began a dramatic shift to the right, pushing forth emergency measures and appointments of well-known conservatives to key positions, remains a mystery.[11] Both the democratic opposition in the USSR and many scholars and pundits in the West at the time believed that Gorbachev had now shown his true colors, that all along he had been only a reluctant reformer, a secret authoritarian. One prominent American historian of Russia told a gathering of senators that the Soviet president was "a front for the KGB." Though it is still impossible to know for certain Gorbachev's motivations, there is reason to believe that the "forces of order"—the army, the KGB, the MVD, conservative Communists and Russian nationalists—had reached the limits of their tolerance for reform by the fall of 1990 and were threatening action, that Gorbachev moved to the right to contain the Right, and that his actions after April 1991 and particularly during the August coup should remove any doubts about his sincere commitment to democratization.

The restructuring of the central government and the increase of power in the hands of Gorbachev in December could not resolve the fundamental political problem in the USSR—the relationships between the center and the peripheries, most importantly the union republics. This problem was daily linked to the underlying problem of the economy. The Ukrainian deputy to the USSR Congress of People's Deputies, V. P. Fokin, told Prime Minister Ryzhkov in December that his government had "been unable to create an effective system for the state administration of the economy. So don't keep us from doing it: Support the republics' striving for independence in the handling of economic questions. If you don't, no forcible pressure, no decrees or incantations will lead to a stabilization of the situation." Ryzhkov replied that an "undeclared war" had been unleashed against the government that aimed "to strike a blow at the state, at the sociopolitical system, and to crush it once and for all." The war was being waged "under the flag of the market." The government, he went on, was in favor of sovereignty for the republics, but also of the sovereignty of the Union as a whole. It was, after all, the government that began transferring prerogatives of the center to the republics. "At the same time, we have always favored the preservation of the Soviet federation's territorial integrity, the preservation of its social choice and single economic space, and the observance of all rights of citizens and peoples throughout the Union."[12]

But Yeltsin and the "democratic movement" claimed that the political logic of the government was to wreck the republics' sovereignty and sabotage radical reforms. "The so-called revolution from above has ended. The Kremlin is no longer the initiator of the country's renewal or an active champion of the new. The processes of renewal, blocked at the level of the center, have moved to the republics. . . . The Union has lost at least six republics as a result of its policy of pressure."[13] Gorbachev called for "firm power" and proposed a referendum on a union of sovereign states. The results in each republic would be a final verdict, and then the law on secession would apply. He stated that he was for "a Union of sovereign states with a new division of authority, but a single state nevertheless."

Tensions increased in mid-December 1990 in the Baltic region. Mysterious explosions occurred in Riga. On January 8, workers marched to the Lithuanian parliament to protest price hikes and demand the resignation of the government. Water cannons dispersed the crowds. The price rises were rescinded, and Prime Minister Prunskiene resigned. Gorbachev called on Lithuania to restore the full force of the USSR and Lithuanian SSR constitutions, but President

Vytautas Landsbergis refused to restore what he labeled the "constitution of invaders" and called for civil disobedience. A pro-Soviet minority movement called for direct presidential rule of Lithuania, and on January 11, a mysterious Committee for National Salvation of Lithuania was announced. That same day, Soviet MVD troops occupied the Vilnius Press House, and shots were fired. Gorbachev responded by dispatching a mediation team from his Council of the Federation, but just after they reached Vilnius, 13 people were killed in the fighting.

Another Committee of National Salvation appeared in Riga, and the pro-Soviet Black Berets, acting on their own but confident of support from the central Ministry of Interior, initiated clashes in which five people were killed. The opposition organized a rally of more than 100,000 people in Moscow on January 20 to protest the events in the Baltic. The democrats were convinced that a coup had been planned in the Baltic, only to be thwarted by resistance and lack of will. Whereas Pugo, who was probably most responsible for the Baltic tragedies, defended the actions in Vilnius as self-defense, Gorbachev both expressed regret at the loss of life and blamed the clashes on the intransigence of the Lithuanians. He ordered, however, that no troops engage in unauthorized activity and that no one be allowed to appeal to the armed forces in the political struggle. Most importantly, Gorbachev did not sanction the armed overthrow of the elected governments of the Baltic republics or respond to the cries from the Right that he institute presidential rule there.

It is probable that to enforce the existing laws and preserve a state that had lost much of its legitimacy, Gorbachev went along with the crackdown in Vilnius in a gamble that a show of force might strengthen his hand both with the conservatives in the center and against the nationalists on the periphery. He had to demonstrate to wary supporters and suspicious opponents, first, that he was able to prevent disintegration and chaos from engulfing the country, and second, that he remained committed to progress toward democracy. His appeals were based on what he considered "constitutional" in the given situation. Paradoxically, the result of the clumsy repression in the Baltic was not the feared end of democratization, but a demonstration of the limited value of bayonets. Whatever the reasons for the actions in the Baltics—and it appears that they were initiated by local pro-Communist groups and sanctioned by the conservatives in the center—they embarrassed Gorbachev internationally and demonstrated the cost of his alliance with the Right.

In the following months, the political polarization of Left and Right left Gorbachev increasingly isolated. His measures to deal with the crisis—the withdrawal of 50- and 100-ruble notes in order to combat inflation, joint patrols of soldiers and policemen in Soviet cities, the crackdown on independent television journalists—led to even more open attacks on him by the opposition. On February 19, 1991, Yeltsin went on central television and called for Gorbachev's resignation. *Pravda* attacked him for his personal ambition, and even the more moderate *Izvestiia* called his speech a mistake. The USSR Supreme Soviet debated the speech and adopted a resolution saying it was unconstitutional and created an emergency situation in the country. Gorbachev struck back at the democratic opposition in a speech in Minsk on February 26. While affirming that he was for political pluralism and democracy, Gorbachev complained that the opposition was moving beyond legality and engaging in a struggle for power that was leading to confrontation. On this occasion, he once again affirmed his own faith in "the socialist option." Gorbachev continued to believe that he could work with his comrades, Yazov and Kryuchkov (head of the KGB), and a reformed Communist party. But conservatives within the upper echelons of the party, particularly in the Central Control Commission, pushed for removal of the leading liberals in the party. The Central Committee plenum at the end of January raised the question of removing Shatalin from its membership. In the next few months, Yakovlev and Shevardnadze were attacked and eventually resigned from the party to form their own democratic political movement.

By March 1991, a stalemate had been reached between Left, Right, and the Gorbachev Center. In the newly elected Security Council, conservatives like Vice President Yanaev, Prime Minister Pavlov, KGB chief Kryuchkov, MVD head Boris Pugo, and Minister of Defense Yazov sat with Gorbachev advisors Evgenii Primakov, Bakatin, and Foreign Minister Bessmertnykh. Two problems were paramount: the failing economy and the breakup of the union. Gorbachev had no real program for the economy but hoped to achieve consensus on the union treaty as a necessary first step toward economic revival. On March 17, a referendum was held throughout the Soviet Union on the question of establishing a union of sovereign republics. 147,000,000 people voted, and 112,000,000 (76.4 percent of those who voted) came out for the union. Six republics (Armenia, Georgia, Moldavia, and the Baltic republics) refused to participate. Russia and others added other questions to the referendum. Though support for Yeltsin was strong in Russia, where his proposal for an elected presidency passed overwhelmingly, Gorbachev could be satisfied with the overwhelming vote for the union. His greatest support came from the countryside and the more conservative republics in Central Asia; he did much less well in the largest cities, Moscow, Leningrad, and Kiev. But he could argue that he now had a mandate for preservation of the Soviet Union as a free association of sovereign republics.

As the crisis intensified in April and as Yeltsin won new powers in the Russian republic, Gorbachev reconsidered this strategy. His turn to the right had effectively restrained the Right for five months but had not halted the drift toward independence in the Baltics, Transcaucasia, and Moldavia. A choice had to be made between armed force and a complete break with the "democrats" on one hand, or accommodation and negotiation with the popular forces on the other. Now, with the Left more popular than ever, Gorbachev shifted once more. On April 23, he met at a dacha at Novo-Ogarevo with Yeltsin and the leaders of eight other republics and hastily worked out an agreement to finalize the draft of the union treaty, prepare a constitution for the union of sovereign states within six months after the signing of the treaty, and carry out new elections for the union political bodies. No overthrow of elected bodies was to be tolerated, the role of union republics was to be radically enhanced, and the center would be reduced to an executive dependent on the wills and revenues of the republics.[14]

All through the period of Gorbachev's alliance with the Right, negotiations had continued between the center and those nine republics willing to work within some form of union over the drafts of a treaty of union. When the first draft was published in November 1990, it was criticized for being too centralist and for not involving the republics sufficiently in its drafting. There was far greater republic participation in the production of the second draft, published on March 9, 1991. The Union was to be a federation, with federal laws supreme, one currency, a federal budget, and taxes. The republics were responsible for setting the rules for secession from the union and accepting new members into the union, whereas the center was to control implementation of security, war and peace, and foreign policy. The overall strategy for state security, the determination of foreign and defense policies, and the compilation and monitoring of the budget, were to be joint responsibilities of the center and the republics, and the ownership of property, resources, and lands was to be shared by center and republics, with republic laws to be considered in implementation of use.

Both the drafting of the union treaty and the referendum indicated that the Soviet Union had divided into two parts:

the independence-minded republics (the Baltic three, Moldavia, Georgia, and Armenia) for whom no form of union was acceptable; and the Muslim-Slavic majority that had voted for union, though the form was yet to be decided. The Novo-Ogarevo agreement meant that Gorbachev had essentially agreed to recognize the sovereignty of all union republics and the right of those who wished to opt out of the union to do so. Though he still faced significant opposition from conservatives who feared that the union treaty conceded far too much power to the republics, Gorbachev managed to tame resistance to the treaty in the USSR Supreme Soviet and to force through a Social Democratic platform in the Central Committee. The actual disarray of the conservatives would be pathetically displaced in their desperate attempt to reverse *perestroika* at the end of August. Gorbachev's strategy had essentially defanged them. The Communist party was deeply divided between those who were prepared to become a real political party and compete in multiparty elections and those who were appalled by Yeltsin's decree to expel the party from institutions and workplaces in the Russian republic and hopeful that they could hold their privileged positions in the state apparatus.

The negotiations for the new union treaty had concluded by August, with plans for the formal signing of the treaty on Wednesday, August 21. Confident that he had saved what he could of the union, Gorbachev left for vacation in the Crimea. On Sunday, August 18, the hastily assembled State Committee for the Emergency ordered Gorbachev's arrest, and the last hope for a Soviet union was destroyed.

After the Coup

Yeltsin's courageous resistance to the coup plotters, strengthened by the fact that he was the legitimate and elected president of the RSFSR, made him the key figure in the reconstruction of political power in the post-coup period. Gorbachev, who had acted resolutely in his private resistance to the coup leaders, denying them any scrap of legitimacy, returned to Moscow severely weakened, without the instruments of power that he had employed before August. The institutions that had constituted the Soviet center— the Communist party, the state bureaucracy, the army, and the police—were all discredited, and the victorious democrats swiftly dismantled what they could.

In the whirlwind set off by the August coup, the fraying fabric of the USSR was finally shredded into 15 independent republics. In response to the vacuum in Moscow and to the emerging power of the Russian republic, the non-Russian states declared their own independence. At the same time, the weakness of many of the republics, most importantly in Central Asia and Transcaucasia, and the economic dependence of the periphery on the center slowed the drift to full separation for a time. A statement of Yeltsin's press officer about rethinking the borders between the Russian republic and its neighbors with Russian diasporas sent a collective shiver through the republics, particularly in Ukraine and Kazakhstan, and forced a retreat to the pragmatic recognition of all existing borders. After some confusion about what could be maintained from the old system, Gorbachev moved quickly to dissolve the Communist party, convinced the Congress of People's Deputies to step aside, and created a loose structure of economic and military coordination for the sovereign republics. His desperate cries, even threats to resign, however, failed to stop the avalanche of independence declarations.

Even as the power of the central state rapidly withered away until the "Soviet Union" was contained within the walls of the Kremlin alone, Gorbachev refused to give up his mission to reconstruct some form of union. The Baltic republics were recognized as fully independent states. In late

September, Armenians voted overwhelmingly for independence. Interrepublic cooperation could only be achieved on
the economic level. In early October, ten republics agreed
to an economic treaty, though only eight actually signed
it on October 18.[15] Early in November, Gorbachev brought
together seven republics—Russia, Belorussia, Kazakhstan,
Kyrgyzstan, Tajikistan, Turkmenistan, and Azerbaijan—in
an agreement to work toward a new confederation, the Union
of Sovereign States.[16] Ominously, the second-largest republic, Ukraine, was absent, preparing for its own referendum
on independence. Within two weeks the effort was scuttled
when the leaders of the seven republics decided to refer the
issue back to their parliaments.[17] On December 1, Ukraine's
citizens voted overwhelmingly for independence, and a week
later, on December 8, the leaders of the three Slavic republics—Yeltsin, Kravchuk, and Shushkevich—announced that
the USSR had ceased to exist and that a commonwealth had
been set up by the three republics that other states were in-
vited to join. Stunned by what he considered an illegal act
and a personal betrayal, Gorbachev protested the foundation
of the commonwealth. But once the Central Asian states,
Armenia, Azerbaijan, and Moldavia agreed to join the commonwealth (*Sodruzhestvo nezavisimykh gosudarstv*), Gorbachev officially resigned, on December 25, 1991, as president of a state that had become a fiction.

The Revenge of the Past

The death of the Soviet Union in its 74th year represented
a failure of Gorbachev's triple revolution. The system fell
because the leadership tried simultaneously to dismantle
the old practices of command in the economic and political
spheres and to construct a democratic multinational federation. Gorbachev's reforms had moved from a "revolution-

from-above" to a massive, multinational series of revolutions from below. Nations formed within the USSR tore that superpower into fragments, each with its own competing interests and aspirations, and Gorbachev's "socialist choice" and supranational ideology fell victim to economic collapse and the rise of powerful nationalisms. A state "socialism" without democracy and a forced modernization without popular consent, all in the multinational context of political and cultural advancement for non-Russians in their own homelands, created nations without full sovereignty. Once it became possible to break the imperial tie with Russia, nationalist leaders moved to take control of the destinies of their own peoples.

The forces of nationalism and localism, which undermined both the former union and Gorbachev's plans for gradual economic and political reform initiated from above, were an understandable reaction to the hypercentralism and bureaucratization of the old system. In the 74 years of Soviet power, the Kremlin had practiced a deeply contradictory policy toward its non-Russian subjects: on the one hand, eliminating real sovereignty and (for the long decades of Stalinism) any semblance of political autonomy; on the other, fostering the development in many republics of native cultures, encouraging education in the local languages, and promoting, through a peculiar form of affirmative action, cadres from the dominant nationality. Industrialization and urbanization, with their Russifying consequences, undermined certain national traditions and created uncertainty about the survival of the non-Russian nations; but the policies of "nativization" (*korenizatsiia* in Russian), the pseudofederal system in which the major nationalities had their own republics, and the growing literacy and mobility from village to town of the non-Russian peoples strengthened the hold of non-Russians on many republics. The result was strengthened nations on the periphery of the empire, not only conscious of their new power before a weakened center but also anxious about their futures in a decaying social and economic system.

When Gorbachev loosened the controls from the center, the effect in the Baltic republics, Armenia, Georgia, Moldavia, and western Ukraine was an explosion of popular nationalism rooted in memories of life without the USSR and a real sense that their cultures, even nature itself, were threatened if they did not strike out on their own. But in most republics, nationalism was accompanied by a desperate grasp for local power by entrenched native elites. In Uzbekistan, Tajikistan, Turkmenistan, and Azerbaijan, the old elites dressed up in nationalist garb to preserve their dominion and suppress democratic movements. Even in those southern republics, like Armenia, Georgia, Kyrgyzstan, and, to a lesser extent, Kazakhstan, where popular democrats were able to remove or reduce the power of the Communists, the deep infrastructure of clan politics remained in place. In Ukraine, Belorussia, and even Russia, former Communists held top political positions and kept their hands firmly on the levers of economic power.

Ernest Gellner and Tom Nairn have emphasized that nationalism is a form of self-defense. In a world chronically unevenly developed, with some nations far ahead in the race for resources, those who are disadvantaged try to find their own way to modernity without falling prey to imperial subordination. The stark legacies of empire—economic dependence on the center and other republics, the incompleteness of state formation in the former Soviet republics, and the intellectual, even emotional, ties to the evaporated union—remain evident in the Commonwealth.

As long as the principal obstacle to self-government and economic revival was the conservative apparatus of central control, sovereignty and independence were potent strategies for renewal, reform, and links to the West. But as they drive toward independence, the republics sometimes work with antiquated notions of sovereignty that have long been superseded by the transnational nature of modern capitalist economies and the hegemonic power of the United States. As Europe evolves toward a new suprastate form of economic and political integration, the constellation of states that we once called the Soviet Union faces fierce competition in a hostile global arena. The choices are harsh in the competitive economic and military environment of the late twentieth century, and the free market is ruthless to the latecomers. After the advantages of disintegration have been exhausted, the need to maximize their limited resources and keep the peace in a fracturing multinational polity may very well lead most of the republics of the former Soviet Union toward a bitter and reluctant acceptance of greater unity. In any case, the future of the non-Russian republics will necessarily involve cautious association, based on pragmatic assessments of real relations of power, with the giant republic of Russia around which the smaller states will continue to orbit.

One powerful strain in the postmortem discussions of Soviet history flows from the conviction that the collapse of the system was implicit in its ideological foundations, which were worked out through the whole evolution and structure of the regime that emerged from the October Revolution.[18] Rather than overdetermining the end of the USSR from its beginning, the interpretation presented in this work begins from different assumptions and moves toward quite different conclusions. Ideology is seen here, not as a fixed recipe book of prescriptions, instructions, or guides, but as an arena of constant contestations between actors and ideas. Even Marxism-Leninism, which acquired in time the hard contours of an official doctrine, proved to be extraordinarily malleable in the hands of Soviet leaders. Whatever its influence may have been as a rough orientation for the embattled

Leninists improvising a new state structure and accommodating themselves to the evident limits placed on their vision by economic underdevelopment, an overwhelmingly
peasant population, and the imperatives of ruling a multinational polity, over time Marxism became both an ex post
facto rationale for choices made by the party and eventually
a meaningless cover for a regime that had little in common
with socialism's original program of egalitarianism, empow-
erment of labor, radical democracy, and internationalism.

The specific and changing contexts in which certain ideas
developed and were employed must be elevated in any historical explanation. From 1917 to 1991, Soviet history dis-
played enormous changes, even reversals, and nowhere was
this more evident than in the policies and developments
among the non-Russian peoples. Here the importance of
state structures and political choices on the development of
relevant communities of association and affiliation can be
seen in the party's unwitting promotion of national consolidation within the bounds of the Soviet imperial arrangement
and Leninist nationality policy. The processes associated
with "modernization"—industrialization, urbanization, increased literacy and social mobility, the emergence of civil
society—had both centrifugal and centripetal effects on the
Soviet peoples. Transforming societies within a set of politically constituted "nations," the Soviet project created
new "national" working classes, intelligentsias, and political elites within republics, while simultaneously encouraging migration into and out of the republics, promoting the
use of Russian, and rewarding those who best adapted to the
new, "modern," Soviet way of life. The differential effects of
Soviet rule on various nationalities ranged from the desta-
bilizing pressures of Russification, demographic and linguistic, in the republics of the West—Ukraine, Belorussia, and
the Baltic—through the more effective consolidation of national cultures in Transcaucasia, to the least transformed

countries of Central Asia, where native political elites and privileged intelligentsias were neither antagonistic one to the other nor particularly confrontational toward Moscow. Yet all non-Russians in the Soviet Union experienced to a greater or lesser degree a gain in their potential capacity to represent themselves as nations. With the authorization from Gorbachev to express their frustrations and discontents, national intelligentsias organized around ethnic symbols to push for a liberating, eventually anti-Communist, agenda. Once popular nationalism overwhelmed the old Communist elites in Lithuania, Armenia, Estonia, and Georgia, nationalism—or at least movements for republic sovereignty, either popular or elite-generated—became irresistible forces.

The collapse of the Soviet Union came at the conjuncture of long-term processes of secular decline and the precipitous program of radical reform set off by Gorbachev. Scholars have long appreciated how Soviet institutions had become petrified during the long reign of Brezhnev, and how disillusion and corruption had become pervasive in the Soviet population. Less well understood was the consolidation of nations within the Soviet federation. But none of these powerful factors necessarily led to an inevitable collapse of the system and the disintegration of the union. The final outcome was contingent on a host of other factors that could have gone differently—among them, the choice to embark on political and economic reform simultaneously; Gorbachev's inability (or unwillingness) to use the power he had to control opposition within the party, society, and the non-Russian republics at an early stage; the determination of many political actors, particularly the Russian and non-Russian intelligentsias, to strike out for even more radical change; and finally, of course, the fateful decision by conservative Communists to launch a coup against Gorbachev.

Though there was no crisis in the Soviet Union in 1985,

the system was in decline, and a small group of determined leaders decided to reverse that trend. The crisis arose with the weakening of political authority and legitimacy, which in turn undermined efforts at economic reform. By 1990–91, the near evaporation of central state power impelled non-Russian elites to scramble for more viable options. Though the referendum of March 1991 showed considerable support for some kind of union, within half a year political realism dictated abandoning the evidently sinking Soviet ship and rowing off in one's own republican rowboat.

The story of Soviet nationalities can be characterized as one of a state making nations, but not just as it pleased.[19] The Soviet state made nations not under circumstances chosen by itself from under those transmitted from the past. Rather than primordial nations slumbering for 74 years, waiting to be aroused by Gorbachev's embrace, the nationalities of the USSR were constantly being shaped by the state-initiated transformation of the Soviet years. Their pasts were constructed and reconstructed; traditions were selected, invented, and enshrined; and even those with the greatest antiquity of pedigree became something quite different from past incarnations. While alternative discourses of affiliation, like class and gender, were silenced, the dominance of the national discourse defined its constituents almost exclusively as subjects of the nation, effacing the multiplicity of possible identities. The empire fell, and nations appeared as new states. How those states will continue the building of their nations, whether as democratic or authoritarian, shaped by tolerant and inclusive or chauvinistic and exclusivist discourses, remains the great open question of our time.

Reference Matter

Notes

Acknowledgments

1. Ronald Grigor Suny, "Nationalities and Nationalism," in Abraham Brumberg, ed., *Chronicle of a Revolution: A Western-Soviet Inquiry into Perestroika* (New York: Pantheon, 1990), pp. 108–28; idem, "Transcaucasia: Cultural Cohesion and Ethnic Revival in a Multinational Society," in Lubomyr Hajda and Mark Beissinger, eds., *The Nationalities Factor in Soviet Politics and Society* (Boulder, Colo.: Westview, 1990), pp. 228–52; idem, "The Revenge of the Past: Socialism and Ethnic Conflict in Transcaucasia," *New Left Review*, no. 184 (Nov.–Dec. 1990): 5–34; idem, "The Soviet South: Nationalism and the Outside World," in Michael Mandelbaum, ed., *The Rise of Nations in the Soviet Union: American Foreign Policy and the Disintegration of the USSR* (New York: Council on Foreign Relations, 1991), pp. 64–88; idem, "Incomplete Revolutions: National Movements and the Collapse of the Soviet Empire," *New Left Review*, no. 189 (Sept.–Oct. 1991): 111–25; idem, "Nationalism and Class in the Russian Revolution: A Comparative Discussion," in Edith Robovin Frankel, Jonathan Frankel, and Baurch Keni-Paz, eds., *Revolution in Russia: Reassessments of 1917* (Cambridge: Cambridge University Press, 1992), pp. 219–46.

Chapter 1

1. Particularly suggestive for this approach to nationality and ethnicity are Ernst Gellner, *Thought and Change* (Chicago: University of Chicago Press, 1964); idem, *Nations and Nationalism*

(Ithaca, N.Y.: Cornell University Press, 1983); Maxime Rodinson, *Cult, Ghetto, and State: The Persistence of the Jewish Question* (London: Al Saqi Books, 1983); Geoff Eley, "Nationalism and Social History," *Social History* 6 (1981): 83–107; Miroslav Hroch, *Die Vorkampfer der nationalen Bewegung bei den kleinen Volkern Europas*, Acta Universitatis Carolinae philosophica et historica 24 (Prague, 1968); idem, *Social Preconditions of National Revival in Europe*, trans. Ben Fowkes (Cambridge: Cambridge University Press, 1985); Benedict Anderson, *Imagined Communities: Reflections on the Origin and Spread of Nationalism* (London: Verso, 1983); and the prolific output of Anthony D. Smith, for example, *The Ethnic Origins of Nations* (Oxford: Basil Blackwell, 1986).

2. Hans Kohn, *The Age of Nationalism* (New York: Harper, 1962); idem, *The Idea of Nationalism*, 2d ed. (New York: Collier-Macmillan, 1967); Carlton J. H. Hayes, "Nationalism," *Encyclopedia of the Social Sciences*, vol. 11 (New York: Macmillan, 1938), pp. 240–49.

3. For a critique on the inadequacy of Marx's thinking on nationalism and an appreciation of the early theorist of nationalism, Friedrich List, see Roman Szporluk, *Communism and Nationalism: Karl Marx Versus Friedrich List* (New York: Oxford University Press, 1988).

4. Tom Nairn, "The Modern Janus," *New Left Review*, no. 94 (Nov.–Dec. 1975): 3–28; idem, *The Break-up of Britain: Crisis and Neo-Nationalism* (London: New Left Review, 1977); Eric J. Hobsbawm, "Some Reflections on 'The Break-up of Britain,'" *New Left Review*, no. 105 (Sept.–Oct. 1977): 3–23. See also the works cited in note 1.

5. The discussion here of the making of nationality and its similarity to the making of class is indebted to what I would call the ethnographic approach of Edward Thompson in his classic work, *The Making of the English Working Class* (London: Victor Golancz, 1963), and to the theorists mentioned above in note 1.

6. Karl W. Deutsch, *Nationalism and Social Communication: An Inquiry into the Foundations of Nationality* (Cambridge, Mass.: MIT Press, 1953), pp. 70–71.

7. Anderson, *Imagined Communities*, p. 40.

8. Ibid., p. 46.

9. Thompson, *English Working Class*, pp. 9–10.

10. Ibid.

11. Joan W. Scott, *Gender and the Politics of History* (New York: Columbia University Press, 1988), p. 5.

12. "What counts as experience is neither self-evident nor straightforward; it is always contested, always therefore political" (Joan W. Scott, "Historicizing 'Experience,'" unpublished paper from the Conference on the Historic Turn in the Human Sciences, University of Michigan, October 5–7, 1990, p. 19). In this paper, Scott argues that experience and language are inseparable and that experience must be historicized rather than seen as fixed, external, or unproblematic. "Experience is, in this approach, not the origin of our explanation, but that which we want to explain" (ibid.).

13. E. Hobsbawm and T. Ranger, eds., *The Invention of Tradition* (Cambridge: Cambridge University Press, 1983).

14. Hroch, *Social Preconditions*, pp. 22–23. As Eley points out, Hroch "pioneers a social-historical approach to the study of nationalist movements and their uneven penetration. In some ways it amounts to a much-needed specification of Deutsch's theory of social communication through the kind of concrete historical investigation that Deutsch himself never really engaged in" (Eley, "Nationalism," p. 101).

15. This useful distinction was made to me by Roman Szporluk.

16. Smith, *Ethnic Origins*, p. 46.

17. Ibid., pp. 21–31.

18. E. J. Hobsbawm, *Nations and Nationalism since 1780: Programme, Myth, Reality* (Cambridge: Cambridge University Press, 1990), chap. 2.

19. Anthony D. Smith, *Theories of Nationalism*, 2d ed. (London: Duckworth, 1983), p. 21.

20. E. Kedourie, *Nationalism* (London: Hutchinson, 1960), p. 1.

21. Gellner, *Nations and Nationalism*, p. 1; Hobsbawm, *Nations and Nationalism*, p. 9. John Breuilly, in *Nationalism and the State* (Manchester: Manchester University Press, 1982), p. 3, lists three basic assertions on which a nationalist argument is based: existence of a nation with an explicit and peculiar character; the priority of the values of the nation over all other interests and values; and the belief that this nation must be as independent as possible, usually requiring the attainment of political sovereignty.

22. The word "interests" is set off by quotation marks here to indicate that rather than being objective and fixed, interests are historically and discursively determined. As Chantal Mouffe argues, "Interests never exist prior to the discourses in which they are articulated and constituted; they cannot be the expression of already existing positions on the economic level" ("Hegemony and

New Political Subjects: Toward a New Concept of Democracy," in Cary Nelson and Lawrence Grossberg, eds., *Marxism and the Interpretation of Culture* [Urbana: University of Illinois Press, 1988], p. 90].

23. This critique of the two-stage model follows the review by Margaret Ramsay Somers ("Workers of the World, Compare," *Contemporary Sociology* 18, no. 3 [May 1989]: 325–29) of Ira Katznelson and Aristide R. Zolberg, eds., *Working-Class Formation: Nineteenth-Century Patterns in Western Europe and the United States* (Princeton: Princeton University Press, 1986). As Somers points out, it is an error to attribute "to class structure a conceptual independence from the formative role of collective action, retaining an a priori directionality from structure to action in the conceptual definition." Action should not be reduced to response. Furthermore, structure should not be reduced to economics. The intervention and contribution to class (and nationality formation) by culture, politics, gender, religion, law, or demography should not be eliminated in favor of a notion of a separate, causally dominant economic sphere.

24. Not all nationalities, of course, are based on pre-existing ethnic communities; they may (like the American or Swiss) be made up of many "ethnicities" and unified around a shared cultural or political ideal. Among Americans, two poles may be imagined in thinking about an American "ethnicity" or nationality. At one extreme are those who define true Americans as only those closest to the original settlers of the United States—white, Protestant northern Europeans—and define the "other" in terms of race, color, or "ethnic" culture. At the other pole are those who conceive of Americans as belonging to a uniquely inclusive nationality based on shared commitment to democratic political principles and tolerance of differences. Ethnicity is underplayed here, and though "race" is accepted as "real," it does not preclude inclusion within the essentially supraethnic community. On defining class and race in the United States, see Barbara Jeanne Fields, "Ideology and Race in American History," in J. Morgan Kousser and James M. McPherson, eds., *Region, Race, and Reconstruction: Essays in Honor of C. Vann Woodward* (Oxford: Oxford University Press, 1982), pp. 143–77; idem, "Slavery, Race and Ideology in the United States of America," *New Left Review*, no. 181 (May–June 1990): 95–118; and David R. Roediger, *The Wages of Whiteness: Race and the Making of the American Working Class* (London: Verso, 1991).

25. The insight about class being more relevant at a local than a national level was first suggested to me by my colleague Kathleen Canning.

26. "Within every society, each social agent is inscribed in a multiplicity of social relations—not only social relations of production, but also the social relations, among others, of sex, race, nationality, and vicinity. All these social relations determine positionalities or subject positions, and every social agent is therefore the locus of many subject positions and cannot be reduced to one. . . . Furthermore, each social position, each subject position, is itself the locus of multiple possible constructions, according to the different discourses that can construct that position. Thus, the subjectivity of a given social agent is always precariously and provisionally fixed or, to use the Lacanian term, sutured at the intersection of various discourses" (Mouffe, "Hegemony," p. 90).

Chapter 2

1. This, indeed, is the argument I have tried to develop in my work on the republics of Transcaucasia. See, for example, Ronald Grigor Suny, *Armenia in the Twentieth Century* (Chico, Calif.: Scholars Press, 1983); idem, *The Making of the Georgian Nation* (Bloomington: Indiana University Press, 1988); idem, "Nationalist and Ethnic Unrest in the Soviet Union," *World Policy Journal* 6, 3 (Summer 1989): 503–28.

2. Ronald Grigor Suny, "Nationalism and Social Class in the Russian Revolution: The Cases of Baku and Tiflis," in Ronald Grigor Suny, ed., *Transcaucasia, Nationalism and Social Change: Essays in the History of Armenia, Azerbaijan, and Georgia* (Ann Arbor: Michigan Slavic Publications, 1983), pp. 239–58; idem, "Tiflis, Crucible of Ethnic Politics, 1860–1905," in Michael F. Hamm, ed., *The City in Late Imperial Russia* (Bloomington: Indiana University Press, 1986), pp. 249–81; idem, *Making of the Georgian Nation*; idem, *The Baku Commune, 1917–1918: Class and Nationality in the Russian Revolution* (Princeton, N.J.: Princeton University Press, 1972).

3. In 1905, Armenians and Azerbaijanis in and around Baku fought and killed each other. In February, Azerbaijanis attacked first, alarmed by rumors of Armenians arming themselves, and Armenians, led by the leading nationalist party, the *Dashnaktsutiun*, retaliated fiercely. A second round of mutual massacre occurred in August. Rioters set fire to the oil fields. Both the Social Democrats

and the oil industrialists worked to reconcile the Armenian and Azerbaijani communities. The passivity of the government inspired suspicions that tsarist authorities had instigated, or at least favored, the riots.

4. Suny, *Baku Commune*, p. 14.

5. Marc Raeff, "Patterns of Russian Imperial Policy Toward the Nationalities," in Edward Allworth, ed., *Soviet Nationality Problems* (New York: Columbia University Press, 1971), p. 23.

6. "The search for effective protection against the unruly inhabitants of the open steppe" went along with a spontaneous spread of peasant agriculture "dialectically determining one another" (Raeff, "Patterns," p. 37).

7. M. K. Rozhkova, *Ekonomicheskaia politika tsarskogo pravitel'stva na srednem vostoke vo vtoroi chetverti XIX veka i russkaia buzhuaziia* (Moscow and Leningrad: Izd. AN SSSR, 1949), pp. 86, 93–95; Firuz Kazemzadeh, "Russian Penetration of the Caucasus," in Taras Hunczak, ed., *Russian Imperialism from Ivan the Great to the Revolution* (New Brunswick, N.J.: Rutgers University Press, 1974), pp. 254–55; Suny, *Making of the Georgian Nation*, pp. 91–92.

8. For the incorporation of the Georgian and Armenian elites into the Russian administration in the Caucasus, see Suny, *Making of the Georgian Nation*, pp. 63–95.

9. David Laitin has developed an elaborate model to explain the rise of nationalism from the variable of "most-favored-lord" status; see his "The National Uprisings in the Soviet Union," *World Politics* 44, 1 (Oct. 1991): 139–77.

10. Hans Rogger, *Jewish Policies and Right-Wing Politics in Imperial Russia* (Berkeley: University of California Press, 1986), p. 26.

11. Anthony L. H. Rhinelander, *Prince Michael Vorontsov, Viceroy to the Tsar* (Montreal: McGill University Press, 1990).

12. For a discussion of tsarist nationality policy during the reign of Alexander III (1881–94), see P. A. Zaionchkovskii, *Rossiiskoe samoderzhavie v kontse XIX stoletiia: (Politicheskaia reaktsiia 80-kh–nachala 90-kh godov* (Moscow: Mysl', 1970), pp. 117–38.

13. For a discussion of tsarist policy and its effects in Ukraine, Belorussia, and Russian Poland, see Theodore Richard Weeks, "The National World of Imperial Russia: Policy in the Kingdom of Poland and Western Provinces, 1894–1914," Ph.D. diss., University of California, Berkeley, 1992.

14. Rogger, *Jewish Policies*, passim.

15. Martha Brill Olcott, *The Kazakhs* (Stanford, Calif.: Hoover Institution Press, 1987), pp. 83–99.

16. Ibid., p. 18. Olcott tends to treat the Kazakhs as a single "nation" after the initial ethnogenesis in the fifteenth and sixteenth centuries, underplaying the divisions into the three *zhuz* ("hundreds," often translated "hordes"). "Although the Russians dealt with the Kazakhs as separate hordes, the Kazakhs continued to view themselves as one people, as is shown by the number of Kazakh legends and tales of a common ancestor" (pp. 11–12).

17. Steven L. Guthier, "The Belorussians: National Identification and Assimilation, 1897–1970," *Soviet Studies* 29, 1 (Jan. 1977): 37, 39.

18. Nicholas P. Vakar, *Belorussia: The Making of a Nation: A Case Study* (Cambridge, Mass.: Harvard University Press, 1956), pp. 29–30.

19. Ibid., pp. 81–82.

20. S. Ahurski, *Ocherki po istorii revoliutsionnogo dvizheniia v Belorussii, 1863–1917* (Minsk, 1928), p. 23; Ivan S. Lubachko, *Belorussia under Soviet Rule, 1917–1957* (Lexington: The Press of the University of Kentucky, 1972), p. 6.

21. "When the February Revolution took place," writes Richard Pipes, "the Belorussian national movement was still in its embryonic stage. There was only one Belorussian political party: the Hromada, which had a very small organized following and was unknown to the masses of the population. . . . There is no evidence that in 1917 the peasantry, which composed the mass of the Belorussian people, possessed any consciousness of ethnic separateness" (Richard Pipes, *The Formation of the Soviet Union: Communism and Nationalism, 1917–1923* [Cambridge, Mass.: Harvard University Press, 1954; reprinted 1964], p. 73).

22. See the documents collected in S. M. Dimanshtein, ed., *Revoliutsiia i natsional'nyi vopros. Dokumenty i materialy po istorii natsional'nogo voprosa v Rossii i SSSR v XX veke* (Moscow: Izdatel'stvo Kommunisticheskoi akademii, 1930), pp. 267–76.

23. Pipes, *Formation of the Soviet Union*, p. 75. At the western front, the Bolsheviks polled 66.9 percent and the SRs 18.5 percent; in Minsk district the parties polled 63.1 percent and 19.8 percent respectively, and the Mensheviks and the Bund took only 1.7 percent and the *Hramada* 0.3 percent. Pipes's statistics are from A. Kirzhnits, "Sto dnei sovetskoi vlasti v Belorussii," *Proletarskaia revoliutsiia*, no. 3/74 (1928): 101–2; V. B. Stankevich, *Sud'by naro-*

dov Rossii (Berlin, 1921), p. 39; V. K. Shcharbakou, *Kastrychnits-kaia revoliutsyia na Belarusi i belapol'skaia okupatsyia* (Minsk, 1930), p. 50.

24. Lubachko, *Belorussia*, pp. 18–25.

25. Guthier, "Belorussians," pp. 49–50.

26. Vakar, *Belorussia*, p. 105.

27. Miroslav Hroch, *Social Preconditions of National Revival in Europe*, trans. Ben Fowkes (Cambridge: Cambridge University Press), pp. 96–97.

28. Dimanshtein, *Revoliutsiia*, p. 260.

29. From the ancient name for eastern Transcaucasia, *Atropatene*, came the Persian form *Ader-badagan*, the Armenian *Atrpatakan*, and the Arab *Aderbaijan* or *Azerbaijan*, which meant "the land of fire," a reference to the fire temples fed by underground sources of natural gas and oil.

30. Suny, *Baku Commune*, p. 14. The dominant groups among the Azerbaijanis were the landlords and the Muslim clergy. The Russian government recognized the Muslim landlords as nobles and sanctioned their right to the land and their hegemony over both Muslim and Armenian peasants. Immediately after the Russian conquest, the properties of the mosques were seized, and clerics faced impoverishment. The Muslim judges (*gadi*) were brought under state supervision (as both the Georgian Orthodox and the Armenian Apostolic churches had been) and Russian laws gradually displaced Muslim law (as they had Georgian and the remnants of Armenian law). Whereas most industrialists were European, Armenian, or Russian, the largest number of small shopkeepers and tradespeople in Baku were Muslim. See Audrey Altstadt-Mirhadi, "The Azerbaijani Turkish Community of Baku Before World War I," Ph.d. diss., University of Chicago, 1983, pp. 18–19, 27–30, 47–49, 175–83.

31. Emblematic of the early scholars and publicists who began the study of the Azeri language were 'Abbas' Qoli Agha Bakikhanov (1794–1846), who wrote histories of the region, and Mirza Fath 'Ali Akhundzada (Akhundov, 1812–78), author of the first Azeri plays. Though eventually these figures would be incorporated into a national narrative as predecessors of the Turkic revival, a variety of conflicting impulses stimulated early Azerbaijani intellectuals. Akhundzada, for example, "epitomized the contradictions inherent in the uncertain identity of an Azerbaijani of his time: A tsarist official of impeccable loyalty, he described himself as 'al-

most Persian' and his philosophical writings reveal the depth of his preoccupation with all things Persian, both good and bad. . . . Nor was he devoid of typically Persian anti-Ottoman sentiments." Tadeusz Swietochowski, *Russian Azerbaijan, 1905−1920: The Shaping of National Identity in a Muslim Community* (Cambridge: Cambridge University Press, 1985), p. 24.

32. Ibid., p. 193.

33. John Armstrong, *Ukrainian Nationalism* (New York: Columbia University Press, 1963), p. 10.

34. Steven L. Guthier, "The Popular Base of Ukrainian Nationalism in 1917," *Slavic Review* 38, 1 (Mar. 1979): 32. In 1897, Ukrainians made up only 35 percent of the population in the 113 towns in Ukraine; the larger the town, the smaller the Ukrainian proportion. In Kiev, Ukrainians made up 22 percent of the population, Russians 54 percent, Jews 12 percent, and Poles 7 percent; in Kharkiv, Ukrainians accounted for 26 percent of the population, Russians 53 percent, Jews 6 percent, and Poles 0.3 percent. Steven L. Guthier, "Ukrainian Cities During the Revolution and the Interwar Era," in Ivan L. Rudnytsky, ed., *Rethinking Ukrainian History* (Edmonton: Canadian Institute of Ukrainian Studies, University of Alberta, 1981), p. 157; Patricia Herlihy, "Ukrainian Cities in the Nineteenth Century," in Rudnytsky, ed., *Rethinking Ukrainian History*, p. 151.

35. On the formation of the Ukrainian literary language, see George Y. Shevelov, "Ukrainian," in Alexander M. Schenker and Edward Stankiewicz, eds., *The Slavic Literary Languages: Formation and Development* (New Haven: Yale Concilium on International and Area Studies, 1980), pp. 143−60.

36. John-Paul Himka, *Galician Villagers and the Ukrainian National Movement in the Nineteenth Century* (Basingstoke, Hampshire: Macmillan, 1988); idem, *Socialism in Galicia: The Origins of Polish Social Democracy and Ukrainian Radicalism (1860−1890)* (Cambridge, Mass.: Harvard Ukrainian Research Institute, 1983).

37. In Austrian Galicia, the economic and political grievances of Ukrainian peasants and the anti-Jewish editorial policy of the leading nationalist newspaper contributed to widespread anti-Semitism. "The Ukrainian nationalism that took root in rural Galicia had a distinctly anti-Jewish component," writes John-Paul Himka in his study, "Ukrainian-Jewish Antagonism in the Galician Countryside During the Late Nineteenth Century," in Peter J. Potichnyj and

Howard Aster, eds., *Ukrainian-Jewish Relations in Historical Perspective* (Edmonton: Canadian Institute of Ukrainian Studies, University of Alberta, 1988), pp. 111–58.

38. On the peasant movement in Right Bank Ukraine (Kiev, Podolia, and Volhynia provinces), see Robert Edelman, *Proletarian Peasants: The Revolution of 1905 in Russia's Southwest* (Ithaca, N.Y.: Cornell University Press, 1987).

39. "Most of the men who undertook the propagation of the national idea in Ukraine were intellectuals with a middle-class background although many of them were of peasant stock. Hrushevsky was the son of an official in the Russian ministry of public instruction, and Dmitro Doroshenko was the son of a military veterinarian. Colonel Eugene Konovalets and Volodimir Naumenko were the sons of teachers. Nicholas Mikhnovsky, Volodimir Chekhovsky, Valentine Sadovsky, Serhi Efremov, and Colonel Peter Bolbochan were the sons of priests" (John Reshetar, *The Ukrainian Revolution, 1917–1920: A Study in Nationalism* [Princeton: Princeton University Press, 1952], pp. 320–21).

40. Ibid., p. 48.

41. See the resolutions of the First Ukrainian Military Congress in May 1917 in Dimanshtein, *Revoliutsiia*, pp. 139–43; Pipes, *Formation*, p. 63; Reshetar, *Ukrainian Revolution*, pp. 50–51, 102n–103n.

42. Reshetar, *Ukrainian Revolution*, pp. 319–23.

43. See particularly the conclusion in Pipes, *Formation*, pp. 283–86.

44. Ibid., p. 149.

45. Guthier, "Popular Base," p. 40.

46. Ibid., p. 46.

47. Ibid., p. 41.

48. Ibid.

49. "The Central Rada and the Directory failed to solve the agricultural problem; the hetman government did worse. It was constantly a step behind the revolutionary spirit of the peasants. Its policy was to carry out the land reform legally for approval by a future Constituent Assembly. For this reason it was not able to compete with the Bolsheviks, who were promising the land to the peasants immediately, or even with Makhno, who was giving the land to the peasants as soon as it was captured. For the peasants, the land was a primary question and those forces that would not interfere in the division of land would get their support" (Michael

Palij, *The Anarchism of Nestor Makhno, 1918–1920: An Aspect of the Ukrainian Revolution* [Seattle: University of Washington Press, 1976], pp. 54–55).

50. For another point of view on Ukrainian nationalism and the peasantry, see Andrew P. Lamis, "Some Observations on the Ukrainian National Movement and the Ukrainian Revolution, 1917–1921," *Harvard Ukrainian Studies* 2, 4 (Dec. 1978): 525–31. Lamis argues that Ukrainian nationalism from Taras Shevchenko on had a dual nature: glorification of the homeland and a demand for social reform. Often these two components remained separate and in a state of dialectical tension (p. 528). He takes issue with Arthur Adams, who claimed that Ukrainian peasants revolted during the German occupation primarily because of the grain requisitions and fear for their land. Lamis contends that the jacquerie was nationalist, aimed toward both national and social freedom, even though the peasants and the intelligentsia did not act in concert (p. 530). For Adams's argument, see his essay, "The Great Ukrainian Jacquerie," in Taras Hunczak, ed., *The Ukraine 1917–1921: A Study in Revolution* (Cambridge, Mass.: Harvard Ukrainian Research Institute, 1977), pp. 247–70.

51. The report, authored by the German writer Collin Ross, was first published in *Arkhiv russkoi revoliutsii* (Berlin: Slovo, 1922–37), 1: 368–76, and translated and reprinted in James Bunyan, *Intervention, Civil War, and Communism in Russia, April-December 1918: Documents and Materials* (Baltimore: The Johns Hopkins University Press, 1936), pp. 4–5.

52. [Colonel Jones], "The Position in the Ukraine," Public Records Office, London, Cab 24/52, ff. 117–18. I would like to thank Professor George Liber for a copy of this document, which was—to my knowledge—first referred to by Professor David Saunders in his paper, "What Makes a Nation a Nation? Ukrainians since 1600," presented at the Conference on Premodern and Modern National Identity, University of London, March 30–April 3, 1989.

53. Adams, "Great Ukrainian Jacquerie," pp. 259–60. See also his *Bolsheviks in the Ukraine: The Second Campaign, 1918–1919* (New Haven: Yale University Press, 1963).

54. In 1897, the population of Vilnius was 40.3 percent Jewish, 30.9 percent Polish, and only 7 percent Lithuanian; Vilnius district, excluding the city, had a population that was 35 percent Lithuanian; the population of the whole province was 56 percent Belorussian and 17.5 percent Lithuanian (Alfred Erich Senn, *The Emer-*

gence of Modern Lithuania [New York: Columbia University Press, 1959], p. 42).

55. By 1913, Estonians made up 69.2 percent of the urban population of Estonia, Russians 11.9 percent, and Germans 11.2 percent. In Tallinn, Estonians were 72 percent of the population, though that figure declined during the war (to 58 percent by 1917) because of the influx of Russian and other workers (Toivo U. Raun, *Estonia and the Estonians* [Stanford, Calif.: Hoover Institution Press, 1987], p. 91). In Riga, Latvians had become a plurality by 1881, and by 1913 they made up 38.8 percent of the city's population, Russians 22.4 percent, and Germans 16.4 percent (Anders Henriksson, "Riga: Growth, Conflict, and the Limitations of Good Government, 1850–1914," in Hamm, ed., *The City*, p. 182).

56. Toivo U. Raun and Andrejs Plakans, "The Estonian and Latvian National Movements: An Assessment of Miroslav Hroch's Model," *Journal of Baltic Studies* 21, 2 (Summer 1990): 133.

57. Ibid., pp. 133–34.

58. Ibid., p. 134.

59. Ibid., p. 136; Hroch, *Social Preconditions*, p. 85.

60. Hroch, *Social Preconditions*, p. 85.

61. Raun, *Estonia*, p. 100.

62. Ibid., p. 101.

63. Ibid., p. 103.

64. I. G. Ozol, "The Revolution in Latvia, 1905–1907," unpublished typescript in the Boris I. Nicolaevsky Collection, Hoover Institution Archives, ser. 67, box 121, folders 1–2, pp. 58, 70–71.

65. Bruno Kalnins, "The Social Democratic Movement in Latvia," in Alexander and Janet Rabinowitch, eds., with Ladis K. D. Kristof, *Revolution and Politics in Russia: Essays in Memory of B. I. Nicolaevsky* (Bloomington: Indiana University Press, 1972), p. 137.

66. Andrew Ezergailis, *The 1917 Revolution in Latvia* (Boulder, Colo.: East European Quarterly, 1974), p. 145; idem, *The Latvian Impact on the Bolshevik Revolution, The First Phase: September 1917 to April 1918* (Boulder, Colo.: East European Monographs, 1983), p. 75.

67. Ezergailis, *Latvian Impact*, pp. 79, 87, 89.

68. For an attempt to deal with the different choices of the Estonians and the Latvians in 1917, see Stanley W. Page, *The Formation of the Baltic States: A Study of the Effects of Great Power Politics upon the Emergence of Lithuania, Latvia, and Estonia*

(Cambridge, Mass.: Harvard University Press, 1959; reprinted New York: Howard Fertig, 1970), pp. 83–85.

69. Although the Georgian Church, like the Orthodox churches of Greece and Russia, maintains the position of the Council of Chaledon (A.D. 451) of "one and the same Christ in two natures without confusion or change, division or separation," the Armenian Church retains a modified monophysite Christology that holds that Christ possesses "one nature united in the Incarnate Word." The Armenian Church rejects the mingling of the two natures of Christ, however, and believes that Christ had "both a divine and a human nature, a complete humanity animated by a rational soul" (Sirarpie Der Nersessian, *The Armenians* [London: Thames and Hudson, 1969], p. 77).

70. Maxime Rodinson, *Cult, Ghetto, and State: The Persistence of the Jewish Question* (London: Al Saqi Books, 1983), pp. 80–81.

71. Smith has made the clearest and most useful distinction between premodern ethnic communities (ethnies) and modern nations while underscoring the continuity between them. He lists five characteristics of an "ideal-typical" ethnie: "A large mass of peasants and artisans in villages and small market towns, subject to various restrictions on their freedom . . . and wedded to local 'folk cultures' . . . influenced loosely by the nearest Great Traditions"; competing urban elites; a tiny stratum of priests who transmit the symbolism of the belief-system to various parts of the population; "a fund of myths, memories, values and symbols"; and processes of communication, transmission, and socialization (Anthony D. Smith, *The Ethnic Origins of Nations* [Oxford: Basil Blackwell, 1986], p. 42).

72. Whereas Armenians called themselves *hai* and their country *Haiastan*, other nations have borrowed the terms derived from the Greek sources, first by Hecataeus of Miletus (c. 550 B.C.), which referred to the *Armenoi*, and from the Persian inscription of Darius I at Behistun that mentioned the country of *Armina*.

73. See Nina Garsoian, "Armenia in the Fourth Century: An Attempt to Redefine the Concepts 'Armenia' and 'Loyalty,'" *Revue des études armeniennes*, n.s. 8 (1971): 341–52.

74. On medieval Georgia, see W.E.D. Allen, *A History of the Georgian People from the Beginning down to the Russian Conquest in the Nineteenth Century* (London: Paul, 1932); David Marshall Lang, *The Georgians* (London: Thames and Hudson, 1966); and Cyril Toumanoff, *Studies in Christian Caucasian History*

(Washington, D.C.: Georgetown University Press, 1963). Georgians did not use their modern word for Georgia (sakartvelo) until the fourteenth century. To the Russians, Georgia is known as Gruziia; to the Armenians as Vrastan; and to the Persians as Gurjistan. From the latter word comes the English word "Georgia," though a popular explanation traces it to St. George, the country's patron.

75. Richard G. Hovannisian, ed., The Armenian Image in History and Literature (Malibu: Undena Publications, 1981).

76. On the formation of the Armenian national intelligentsia, see the articles by George A. Bournoutian, Ronald G. Suny, Sarkis Shmavonian, Vahe Oshagan, and Gerard J. Libaridian in Armenian Review 36, 3–143 (Autumn 1983). On the Georgians, see James William Robert Parsons, "The Emergence and Development of the National Question in Georgia, 1801–1921," Ph.d. diss., University of Glasgow, 1987; and Suny, "The Emergence of Political Society in Georgia," in Suny, ed., Transcaucasia, pp. 109–40.

77. Louise Nalbandian, The Armenian Revolutionary Movement: The Development of Armenian Political Parties Through the Nineteenth Century (Berkeley: University of California Press, 1963); Anahide Ter Minassian, Nationalism and Socialism in the Armenian Revolutionary Movement (1887–1912) (Cambridge, Mass.: Zoryan Institute, 1984); Ronald Grigor Suny, "Populism, Nationalism, and Marxism: The Origins of Revolutionary Parties among the Armenians of the Caucasus," Armenian Review 32, 2–126 (June 1979): 134–51; and idem, "Marxism, Nationalism, and the Armenian Labor Movement in Transcaucasia, 1890–1903," Armenian Review 33, 1–129 (Mar. 1980): 30–47. On the Georgians, see D. M. Lang, A Modern History of Soviet Georgia (New York: Grove Press, 1962).

78. Risto Alapuro, State and Revolution in Finland (Berkeley: University of California Press, 1988), p. 90.

79. Anthony F. Upton, The Finnish Revolution 1917–1918 (Minneapolis: University of Minnesota Press, 1980), p. 3.

80. Ibid., p. 29.

81. Hroch, Social Preconditions, p. 74.

82. Alapuro, State and Revolution, p. 34.

83. Ibid., p. 49.

84. Pertti Haapala, "How Was the Working Class Formed? The Case of Finland, 1850–1920," Scandinavian Journal of History 12 (1987): 181–82.

85. Ibid., pp. 188–89, 190.

86. Ibid., p. 183.

87. On the centrality of the *Kalevala* in the construction of Finnish identity, see Tracy X. Karner, "Ideology and Nationalism: The Finnish Move to Independence, 1809–1918," *Ethnic and Racial Studies* 14, 2 (Apr. 1991): 152–69. The *Kalevala* is available in English translation: Eino Friberg, trans., *The Kalevala* (Helsinki: Otava, 1988).

88. On the cooperation of Finnish liberals and the Russian Bolsheviks in 1905 in trying to stimulate an uprising in St. Petersburg, see Antti Kujala, "The Russian Revolutionary Movement and the Finnish Opposition, 1905: The John Grafton Affair and the Plans for an Uprising in St. Petersburg," *Scandinavian Journal of History* 5 (1980): 257–75.

89. Alapuro, *State and Revolution*, p. 127.

90. Upton, *The Finnish Revolution*, p. 37.

91. Ibid., p. 137.

92. Alapuro, *State and Revolution*, pp. 195, 177.

93. Upton, *The Finnish Revolution*, pp. 534–35.

94. The best account of Transcaucasian politics during the revolution and civil war remains Firuz Kazemzadeh, *The Struggle for Transcaucasia (1917–1921)* (New York: Philosophical Library, 1951).

95. For a review of Western writing on 1917 in Russia proper that emphasizes the importance of deep social polarization as an explanation for Bolshevik victory, see Ronald Grigor Suny, "Toward a Social History of the October Revolution," *American Historical Review* 88, 1 (Feb. 1983): 31–52.

96. Geoff Eley, "Remapping the Nation: War, Revolutionary Upheaval and State Formation in Eastern Europe, 1914–1923," in Potichnyj and Aster, eds., *Ukrainian-Jewish Relations*, pp. 205–46.

97. Ibid., p. 232.

Chapter 3

1. E. H. Carr, *The Bolshevik Revolution, 1917–1923*, vol. 3 (London: Macmillan, 1953), pp. 234–235.

2. "We say to the Ukrainians: as Ukrainians, you can run your own lives as you wish. But we extend a fraternal hand to the Ukrainian workers and say to them: together with you we will fight against your and our bourgeoisie. Only a socialist alliance of laborers of all countries eliminates any ground for national persecution

and fighting." V. I. Lenin, *Polnoe sobranie sochinenii* (henceforth *PSS*) (Moscow: Gosizpolit, 1959–), 116.

3. From the brochure *Zadachi proletariata v nashei revoliutsii* *(Proekt platformy proletarskoi partii),* written in April 1917, first published in September. Lenin, *PSS* 31: 167–68.

4. Richard Pipes, *The Formation of the Soviet Union: Communism and Nationalism, 1917–1923* (Cambridge, Mass.: Harvard University Press, 1954; reprinted 1964), p. 11.

5. *Vosmoi s"ezd RKP (b). Mart 1919 goda. Protokoly* (Moscow: Gosizpolit, 1959), pp. 46–48.

6. Ibid., pp. 52–56.

7. Ibid., pp. 397–98.

8. Lenin, *PSS* 50: 20; idem, *Collected Works* (London: Lawrence and Wishart, 1960–), 30:271.

9. Richard G. Hovannisian, "Armenia and the Caucasus in the Genesis of the Soviet-Turkish Entente," *International Journal of Middle East Studies* 4 (1973): 147.

10. Ibid., pp. 15, 27.

11. *Second Congress of the Communist International: Minutes of the Proceedings,* 2 vols. (London: New Park, 1977), 1: 11.

12. "Pervonachal'nyi nabrosok tezisov po natsional'nomu i kolonial'nomu voprosam," Lenin, *PSS* 41: 161–68.

13. In a letter of June 12, 1920, Stalin told Lenin that he ought to include the idea of confederation as the transition step bringing different nations into a single political unit. The Soviet federation (RSFSR) was appropriate for the nationalities that had been part of the old Russia, but not for those which had been independent. He noted that differences between the federative relations within the RSFSR and between the RSFSR and other soviet republics did not exist or were so few that they meant nothing (*net, ili ona tak mala, chto ravniaetsia nuliu;* Lenin, *PSS* 41: 513). This idea was later brought up in Stalin's notion of autonomization. (Stalin's letter is available in an English translation in Xenia Joukoff Eudin and Robert C. North, *Soviet Russia and the East, 1920–1927: A Documentary Survey* [Stanford, Calif.: Stanford University Press, 1957], pp. 67–68.)

14. M. N. Roy, *M. N. Roy's Memoirs* (Bombay: Allied Publishers, 1964), p. 379.

15. Ibid., p. 380.

16. *Second Congress of the Communist International,* 1: 117.

17. Ibid., 1: 110–12. Though Roy himself later underlined Lenin's

shift toward his position, a comparison of his original draft and his theses as presented at the Congress show a significant adjustment on Roy's part as well. Before the Congress, Roy had taken a more forthright position on the primacy of the extra-European revolution, writing: "The fountainhead from which capitalism draws its main strength is no longer to be found in the industrial countries, but in the colonial possessions and dependencies." The European bourgeoisie, he argued, could sacrifice "the entire surplus value in the home country so long as it continues in the position to gain its huge superprofits in the colonies." Thus, the fate of the West was being determined in the East. In his Supplementary Theses at the Congress, he softened this assertion: "European capitalism draws its strength *in the main* not so much from the industrial countries of Europe as from its colonial possessions" (Sibnarayan Ray, ed., *Selected Works of M. N. Roy, Volume I, 1917–1922* [Delhi and New York: Oxford University Press, 1987], pp. 165–66; *Second Congress of the Communist International*, 1: 116; italics added for emphasis). Or in another translation: "One of the main sources from which European capitalism draws its chief strength is to be found in the colonial possessions and dependencies" (*Selected Works of M. N. Roy, Volume I, 1917–1922*, p. 174).

18. Victor Kiernan, "State and Nation in Western Europe," *Past and Present* 30–32 (1965): 20.

19. Ernest Gellner, *Nations and Nationalism* (Ithaca, N.Y.: Cornell University Press, 1983), p. 4.

20. Henry Patterson, "Neo-Nationalism and Class," *Social History* 13, 3 (Oct. 1988): 347.

21. Ibid., p. 246.

22. Weber, *Peasants into Frenchmen: The Modernization of Rural France, 1870–1914* (Stanford, Calif.: Stanford University Press, 1976).

23. Bohdan Krawchenko, *Social Change and National Consciousness in Twentieth-Century Ukraine* (Edmonton: Canadian Institute of Ukrainian Studies, University of Alberta, 1987), p. 64.

24. Ibid., pp. 46–47.

25. "Clan, village, and aul authorities simply reconstituted themselves as soviets and governed their population much as before" (Martha Brill Olcott, *The Kazakhs* [Stanford: Hoover Institution Press, 1987], p. 162).

26. Georg Von Rauch, *The Baltic States, The Years of Indepen-*

dence: Estonia, Latvia, Lithuania 1917–1940 (Berkeley: University of California Press, 1974), pp. 82, 85.

27. Al'bert Pavlovich Nenarokov, "Iz opyta natsional'noiazykovoi politiki pervykh let sovetskoi vlasti," *Istoriia SSSR* 2 (1990): 3–14.

28. Krawchenko, *Social Change*, p. 89.

29. Gerhard Simon, *Nationalism and Policy Toward the Nationalities in the Soviet Union: From Totalitarian Dictatorship to Post-Stalinist Society* (Boulder, Colo.: Westview, 1991), p. 31.

30. Ibid., p. 48.

31. Ibid., p. 51.

32. The struggle between Lenin and Stalin over the nationality question has been extensively explored. See, for example, Pipes, *Formation*, pp. 271–82; Moshe Lewin, *Lenin's Last Struggle* (New York: Pantheon Books, 1968); R. G. Suny, *The Making of the Georgian Nation* (Bloomington: Indiana University Press, 1988), pp. 208–21.

33. Zvi Y. Gitelman, *Jewish Nationality and Soviet Politics: The Jewish Sections of the CPSU, 1917–1930* (Princeton: Princeton University Press, 1972); Bohdan Krawchenko, *Social Change*; James E. Mace, *Communism and the Dilemmas of National Liberation: National Communism in Soviet Ukraine, 1918–1933* (Cambridge, Mass.: Harvard Ukrainian Research Institute, 1983); George Liber, "Urban Growth and Ethnic Change in the Ukrainian SSR, 1923–1933," *Soviet Studies* 41, 4 (Oct. 1989): 574–91.

34. Krawchenko, p. 50.

35. Ibid., p. 56.

36. I. V. Stalin, "Otchetnyi doklad XVII s"ezdu partii o rabote TsK VKP (b), 26 ianvaria 1934 g.," *Sochineniia*, 13 vols. (Moscow: Gosizpolit, 1946–52), 13: 361–62.

37. The famine, which was manmade, has been interpreted by some scholars as a deliberately ethnocidal policy against Ukrainians in particular, rather than as a consequence of the collectivization drive. Though evidence for a policy of genocide is lacking, the argument supporting this view can be found in Robert Conquest, *The Harvest of Sorrow: Soviet Collectivization and the Terror-Famine* (Oxford: Oxford University Press, 1986); and in James E. Mace, "Famine and Nationalism in Soviet Ukraine," *Problems of Communism* 33, 3 (May–June 1984): 37–50.

38. Olcott, *Kazakhs*, pp. 179–87.

39. Ibid., pp. 46–47.

40. On the deportations of about one million people—among them the Chechens, Ingush, Balkars, Karachai, Kalmyks, Crimean Tatars, and Volga Germans—see Aleksandr M. Nekrich, *The Punished Peoples: The Deportation and Tragic Fate of Soviet Minorities at the End of the Second World War*, trans. George Saunders (New York: W. W. Norton, 1978).

41. *Naselenie SSSR: Po dannym vsesoiuznoi perepisi naseleniia 1979 g.* (Moscow: Izpolit, 1980), p. 23; A. M. Khazanov, "The Current Ethnic Situation in the USSR: Perennial Problems in the Period of 'Restructuring,'" *Nationalities Papers* 16, 2 (Fall 1988): 148–49.

42. In Georgia, for example, the Communist party was 76.1 percent Georgian in membership in 1970, though in that year Georgians made up only 66.8 percent of the republic's population. Armenians made up 9.7 percent of the population, but only 8.0 percent of party membership; Russians comprised 8.5 percent of the population and 5.5 percent of the party. *Kommunisticheskaia partiia Gruzii v tsifrakh (1921–1970 gg.) Sbornik statisticheskikh materialov* (Tbilisi: Partiis Istoriis Instituti, 1971), p. 265; J. A. Newth, "The 1970 Soviet Census," *Soviet Studies* 24, 2 (Oct. 1972): 215. At the same time, ethnic Georgians accounted for 82.6 percent of the students in higher education in the republic, whereas Russians made up only 6.8 percent and Armenians 3.6 percent (Richard B. Dobson, "Georgia and the Georgians," in Zev Katz, Rosemarie Rogers, and Frederic Harned, eds., *Handbook of Major Soviet Nationalities* [New York: Free Press, 1975], p. 177).

43. Alexandre Bennigsen, "Several Nations or One People," *Survey*, no. 108 (1979): 51ff.; Michael Rywkin, *Moscow's Muslim Challenge: Soviet Central Asia* (Armonk, N.Y.: M. E. Sharpe, 1982), p. 118. Bennigsen predicted (wrongly, I believe) that for Soviet Muslims the national—the allegiance to the national Soviet republics—was the weakest loyalty, whereas the supranational—allegiance to the Islamic community of Central Asia as a whole—was the strongest.

44. Tom Nairn, "Beyond Big Brother," *New Statesman and Society* 3, 105 (June 15, 1990): 31.

45. On Kazakhstan, see Olcott, *Kazakhs*.

46. Gregory J. Massell, *The Surrogate Proletariat: Moslem Women and Revolutionary Strategies in Soviet Central Asia, 1919–1929* (Princeton: Princeton University Press, 1974), p. 83.

47. Ibid., p. 397.

48. Orlando Figes, *Peasant Russia, Civil War: The Volga Countryside in Revolution, 1917–1921* (Oxford: Oxford University Press, 1989).

49. Olcott, *Kazakhs*, pp. 172–73.

50. Tamara Dragadze, *Rural Families in Soviet Georgia: A Case Study in Ratcha Province* (London: Routledge, 1988), p. 199.

51. Ibid., pp. 137–38.

52. Gerald Mars and Yochanan Altman, "The Cultural Bases of Soviet Georgia's Second Economy," *Soviet Studies* 35, 4 (Oct. 1983): 546–60.

53. S. P. Poliakov, *Traditsionalizm v sovremennom sredneaziatskom obshchestve* (Moscow: Znanie, 1989), p. 100.

54. Mars and Altman, "Cultural Bases," pp. 546–60.

55. Tamara Dragadze, "Family Life in Georgia," *New Society* (Aug. 19, 1976).

56. Massell, *Surrogate Proletariat*, p. 409.

57. Ibid., p. 60.

58. From 1954 to 1973, Armenia's Communist party had both first and second secretaries who were Armenian. Of the union republics only Ukraine, Belorussia, and Estonia (to 1971) also enjoyed this privilege. All other republics had a native first secretary and a Russian or other Slav as second secretary. Georgia lost its native second secretary in 1956, Azerbaijan in 1957. "The dyarchy of native first secretary and Russian second secretary in charge of cadres is now the norm," wrote John H. Miller in 1977. "This is not the same as a strengthening of institutional procedures, in an area, where, before 1953, equivalent functions would have been performed by the security police." John H. Miller, "Cadres Policy in Nationality Areas—Recruitment of CPSU First and Second Secretaries in Non-Russian Republics of the USSR," *Soviet Studies* 39, 1 (Jan. 1977): 35.

59. Yaroslav Bilinsky, "Mykola Skypnyk and Petro Shelest: An Essay on the Persistence and Limits of Ukrainian National Communism," in Jeremy Azrael, ed., *Soviet Nationality Policies and Practices* (New York: Praeger, 1978), pp. 105–43.

60. Mars and Altman, "Cultural Bases," p. 549.

61. One of the fullest compilations on illegal protest movements in the Brezhnev period is Ludmilla Alexeyeva, *Soviet Dissent: Contemporary Movements for National, Religious, and Human Rights*, trans. Carol Pearce and John Glad (Middletown, Conn.: Wesleyan University Press, 1985).

62. The new article in the constitution was to have read: "The Georgian Republic ensures the use of the Georgian language in state and public agencies and in cultural and other institutions and . . . , on the basis of equality, ensures the free use in all these agencies and institutions of Russian, as well as other languages used by the population." *Zaria vostoka*, April 15, 1978, in *Current Digest of the Soviet Press* 30, 17 (May 24, 1978): 12.

63. A full treatment of the Helsinki Watch Committees in Transcaucasia can be found in Yaroslav Bilinsky and Tonu Parming, *Helsinki Watch Committees in the Soviet Union: Implications for the Soviet Nationality Question*, Final Report to the National Council for Soviet and East European Research, 1980. See also Alexeyeva, *Soviet Dissent*.

64. One of the most notable was Zviad Gamsakhurdia, an early advocate of human rights in Georgia, later the first elected chairman of the Supreme Soviet of Georgia and president of the independent Georgian republic. As leader of the nationalist movement in Georgia in the Gorbachev period, Gamsakhurdia opposed the return of the Meskhetian Turks to Georgia and promoted a Georgia for the Georgians. His chauvinistic and authoritarian policies led to a revolt against the president by many of his former sympathizers in December 1991.

Chapter 4

1. Martha Brill Olcott, "Gorbachev's Nationalities Policy and Central Asia," in Rajan Menon and Daniel N. Nelson, eds., *Limits to Soviet Power* (Lexington, Mass.: Lexington Books, 1989), pp. 69–70.

2. The roots of the national crisis in the Transcaucasian republics are explored in my essay, "The Revenge of the Past: Socialism and Ethnic Conflict in Transcaucasia," *New Left Review*, no. 184 (Nov.–Dec. 1990): 5–34.

3. Such a view has been expressed by Richard Pipes, Marshall Goldman, Peter Reddaway, and Alain Besancon, among others.

4. Such a view has been expressed by Stephen Cohen, George Kennan, and Jerry Hough, among others. In *The Gorbachev Phenomenon: A Historical Interpretation* (Berkeley: University of California Press, 1988), Moshe Lewin writes: "The USSR is entering its new age and trying to recover what it missed or mishandled in previous stages, for example, the bourgeois-democratic revolution

of March 1917 and the socialist promises of the October Revolution. The conditions may now be ripe or ripening for the system to reclaim some of the hopes of its idealistic revolutions" (p. 151).

5. Seweryn Bialer, "Gorbachev's Move," in Ferenc Feher and Andrew Arato, eds., *Gorbachev—The Debate* (Atlantic Highlands, N.J.: Humanities Press International, 1989), pp. 38–60; Cornelius Castoriadis, "The Gorbachev Interlude," in Feher and Arato, eds., *Gorbachev*, pp. 61–83.

6. *The New York Times*, November 28, 1988.

7. David B. Nissman, *The Soviet Union and Iranian Azerbaijan: The Use of Nationalism for Political Penetration* (Boulder, Colo.: Westview, 1987). The response from Iranian Azerbaijanis, who had long suffered from the anti-Azerbaijani policies of both the Pahlevi and the Khomeini regimes, was tepid. With schooling in Azeri forbidden for decades, a national consciousness had not developed as in the north.

8. In the Soviet political spectrum, the terms "Left" or "Right," "conservative" or "liberal" in the Gorbachev years are rather like mirror images: the Left proposes greater marketization and dismantling of the institutionalized power of the Communist party, whereas the Right favors maintenance of as much of the old economic and political order as possible. The Left/Right designation is determined not by the content of programs, but by the degree of commitment to radical and rapid change from the post-Stalinist status quo toward a democratic polity and a market economy.

9. *Komsomol'skaya pravda*, January 22, 1991, in *Current Digest of the Soviet Press* 43, 5 (Mar. 6, 1991): 1–4.

10. *Izvestiia*, December 1, 1990.

11. Aleksandr Yakovlev, one of Gorbachev's most radical advisors, was hounded from his position in the party. Vadim Bakatin, the liberal Minister of Internal Affairs, was replaced by the hardliner Boris Pugo. Eduard Shevardnadze surprised the world with his emotional resignation as foreign minister and his warning that a "dictatorship is coming." Nikolai Ryzhkov was replaced as prime minister by the conservative economist Vladimir Pavlov.

12. *Izvestiia*, December 20, 1990, in *Current Digest of the Soviet Press* 43, 52 (Jan. 30, 1991): 3–4.

13. Ibid., pp. 4–5.

14. For an excellent discussion of the April *povorot* (reversal or overturn) that emphasizes the fragility of the democratic opposition to Gorbachev in the winter of 1990–91, see Abraham Brumberg,

"Russia after Perestroika," *New York Review of Books* 38, 12 (June 27, 1991): 53–62.

15. The five Central Asian republics were joined by the RSFSR, Armenia, and Belorussia. Ukraine and Moldavia signed the economic treaty on November 5.

16. *The New York Times*, November 15, 1991.

17. *The New York Times*, November 26, 1991.

18. See, for example, Martin Malia ["Z"], "To the Stalin Mausoleum," *Daedalus* 119, 1 (Winter 1990): 295–344.

19. This paraphrase of Marx's famous statement on "men making their own history" was suggested to me by Professor Charles Lipson of the University of Chicago.

For Further Reading

Allworth, Edward, ed. *Central Asia: A Century of Russian Rule.* New York: Columbia University Press, 1967.

Bennigsen, Alexandre A., and Enders S. Wimbush. *Muslim National Communism in the Soviet Union: A Revolutionary Strategy for the Colonial World.* Chicago: University of Chicago Press, 1979.

Carrère d'Encausse, Hélène. *The Great Challenge: Nationalities and the Bolshevik State, 1917–1930.* Translated by Nancy Festinger. New York: Holmes and Meier, 1991. Originally published as *Le Grand Defi: Bolcheviks et nations, 1917–1930.* Paris: Flammarion, 1987.

Connor, Walker. *The National Question in Marxist-Leninist Theory and Strategy.* Princeton: Princeton University Press, 1984.

Conquest, Robert, ed. *Soviet Nationalities Policy in Practice.* Praeger Publications in Russian History and World Communism, vol. 199. New York: Frederick A. Praeger, 1967.

Danber, Rachel. *The Soviet Nationality Reader: The Disintegration in Context.* Boulder, Colo.: Westview, 1992.

Gitelman, Zvi Y. *Jewish Nationality and Soviet Politics: The Jewish Sections of the CPSU, 1917–1930.* Princeton: Princeton University Press, 1972.

Goldhagen, Erich, ed. *Ethnic Minorities in the Soviet Union.* New York: Praeger, 1968.

Guthier, Steven L. "The Popular Base of Ukrainian Nationalism in 1917." *Slavic Review* 38, 1 (Mar. 1979): 30–47.

Hajda, Lubomyr, and Mark Beissinger, eds. *The Nationalities Fac-*

tor in Soviet Politics and Society. The John M. Olin Critical Issues Series. Boulder, Colo.: Westview, 1990.

Hodnett, Grey. *Leadership in the Soviet National Republics.* Oakville, Ontario: Mosaic, 1978.

Hovannisian, Richard G. *Armenia on the Road to Independence, 1918.* Berkeley: University of California Press, 1967.

———. *The Republic of Armenia.* 2 vols. Berkeley: University of California Press, 1971, 1982.

Humphrey, Caroline. *Karl Marx Collective: Economy, Society, and Religion in a Siberian Collective Farm.* Cambridge: Cambridge University Press, 1983.

Karklins, Rasma. *Ethnic Relations in the USSR: The Perspective from Below.* Boston: Unwin Hyman, 1986.

Katz, Zev, Rosemarie Rogers, and Frederic Harned, eds. *Handbook of Major Soviet Nationalities.* New York: Free Press, 1975.

Kazemzadeh, Firuz. *The Struggle for Transcaucasia (1917–1921).* New York: Philosophical Library, 1951.

Kozlov, Viktor. *The Peoples of the Soviet Union.* Bloomington: Indiana University Press, 1988.

Krawchenko, Bohdan. *Social Change and National Consciousness in Twentieth-Century Ukraine.* London: Macmillan, 1985.

Livezeanu, Irina. "Moldavia, 1917–1990: Nationalism and Internationalism Then and Now." *Armenian Review* 43, nos. 2–3 (170–71) (Summer/Autumn 1990): 153–93.

Lowy, Michael. "Marxists and the National Question." *New Left Review* 96 (Mar.–Apr. 1976): 81–100.

Lubin, Nancy. *Labour and Nationality in Soviet Central Asia.* Princeton: Princeton University Press, 1984.

Mace, James E. *Communism and the Dilemmas of National Liberation: National Communism in Soviet Ukraine, 1918–1933.* Cambridge, Mass.: Harvard Ukrainian Research Institute, 1983.

Mandelbaum, Michael, ed. *The Rise of Nations in the Soviet Union: American Foreign Policy and the Disintegration of the USSR.* New York: Council on Foreign Relations, 1991.

Massell, Gregory J. *The Surrogate Proletariat: Moslem Women and Revolutionary Strategies in Soviet Central Asia, 1919–1929.* Princeton: Princeton University Press, 1974.

Matossian, Mary Kilbourne. *The Impact of Soviet Policies in Armenia.* Leiden: E. J. Brill, 1962.

Motyl, Alexander J. *Sovietology, Rationality, Nationality: Coming to Grips with Nationalism in the USSR.* New York: Columbia University Press, 1990.

Nahaylo, Bohdan, "Nationalities." In Martin McCauley, ed., *The Soviet Union under Gorbachev*, pp. 73–96. London: Macmillan, 1987.

Nekrich, Aleksandr M. *The Punished Peoples: The Deportation and Tragic Fate of Soviet Minorities at the End of the Second World War*. Translated by George Saunders. New York: W. W. Norton, 1978.

Nove, Alec, and J. A. Newth. *The Soviet Middle East: A Model for Development?* London: George Allen and Unwin, 1967.

Olcott, Martha Brill. *The Kazakhs*. Stanford: Hoover Institution Press, 1987.

Pinkus, Benjamin. *The Jews of the Soviet Union: The History of a National Minority*. Cambridge: Cambridge University Press, 1988.

Pipes, Richard. *The Formation of the Soviet Union: Communism and Nationalism, 1917–1923*. Cambridge, Mass.: Harvard University Press, 1954; reprinted 1964.

Rakowska-Harmstone, Teresa. *Russia and Nationalism in Central Asia: The Case of Tadzhikistan*. Baltimore: The Johns Hopkins University Press, 1970.

———. "The Dialectics of Nationalism in the USSR." *Problems of Communism* 23, 3 (May–June 1974): 1–22.

Raun, Toivo U. *Estonia and the Estonians*. Stanford: Hoover Institution Press, 1987.

Rorlich, Azade-Ayse. *The Volga Tatars: A Profile in National Resilience*. Stanford: Hoover Institution Press, 1986.

Rywkin, Michael. *Moscow's Muslim Challenge*. Armonk, N.Y.: M. E. Sharpe, 1982.

Serbyn, Roman, and Bohdan Krawchenko, eds. *Famine in Ukraine, 1932–1933*. The Canadian Library in Ukrainian Studies. Edmonton, Alberta: Canadian Institute of Ukrainian Studies, 1986.

Simon, Gerhard. *Nationalism and Policy Toward the Nationalities in the Soviet Union: From Totalitarian Dictatorship to Post-Stalinist Society*. Translated by Karen Forster and Oswald Forster. Boulder, Colo.: Westview, 1991.

Szporluk, Roman. *Communism and Nationalism: Karl Marx Versus Friedrich List*. New York: Oxford University Press, 1988.

Suny, Ronald Grigor. *The Baku Commune, 1917–1918: Class and Nationality in the Russian Revolution*. Princeton: Princeton University Press, 1972.

———, ed. *Transcaucasia, Nationalism and Social Change: Essays in the History of Armenia, Azerbaijan, and Georgia*. Ann Arbor: Michigan Slavic Publications, 1983.

———. *The Making of the Georgian Nation*. Bloomington: Indiana University Press, 1988; published in association with the Hoover Institution Press.

———. "Nationalities and Nationalism." In Abraham Brumberg, ed., *Chronicle of a Revolution: A Western-Soviet Inquiry into Perestroika*, pp. 108–28. New York: Pantheon, 1990.

———. *Looking Toward Ararat: Armenia in Modern History*. Bloomington: Indiana University Press, 1993.

Swietochowski, Tadeusz. *Russian Azerbaijan, 1905–1920: The Shaping of National Identity in a Muslim Community*. Cambridge: Cambridge University Press, 1985.

Vakar, Nicholas P. *Belorussia, The Making of a Nation: A Case Study*. Cambridge, Mass.: Harvard University Press, 1956.

Vardys, V. Stanley. *The Catholic Church, Dissent, and Nationality in Soviet Lithuania*. New York: Columbia University Press, 1978.

Index

In this index an "f" after a number indicates a separate reference on the next page, and an "ff" indicates separate references on the next two pages. A continuous discussion over two or more pages is indicated by a span of page numbers, e.g., "pp. 57–58." *Passim* is used for a cluster of references in close but not consecutive sequence.

Library of Congress Cataloging-in-Publication Data

Suny, Ronald Grigor.
   The revenge of the past : nationalism, revolution, and the
collapse of the Soviet Union / Ronald Grigor Suny.
     p.   cm.
   Includes bibliographical references and index.
   ISBN 0-8047-2134-3 (alk. paper) :
   ISBN 0-8047-2247-1 (pbk. : alk. paper) :
     1. Soviet Union—History.   2. Nationalism—Soviet Union.
   I. Title.
   DK266.3.S86   1993
   320.5'4'0947—dc20
   93-10373   CIP

⊗ This book is printed on acid-free paper.